Rosemary

This book is dedicated to all my very good friends.

Rosemary
Castle Cook

Recipes from Rosemary Shrager's
Cookery School on the Isle of Harris

Photographs by
Christopher Simon Sykes

Text by Rosemary Shrager
and Sue Gaisford

EVERYMAN

Rosemary, Castle Cook
Recipes from Rosemary Shrager's Cookery School
on the Isle of Harris

Published by Everyman Publishers Plc, London

Text by Rosemary Shrager and Sue Gaisford
Photographs by Christopher Simon Sykes

Designed by Broadbase

© 2001 Everyman Publishers Plc
Text copyright © Rosemary Shrager and Sue Gaisford
Photographs © Christopher S. Sykes / The Interior
Archive

Everyman Publishers Plc
Gloucester Mansions
140A Shaftesbury Avenue
London WC2H 8HD
books@everyman.uk.com

ISBN 1 84159 049 5

Printed and colour separated in the E.U.

Contents

Rosemary is a very courageous woman always striving for perfection. She has an instinctive feel and passion for both finding and respecting the best raw ingredients. I know that Rosemary is one of the very best, and that her natural modesty as well as her relentless search for perfection are a gift of God.

She is also a great teacher with a tremendous ability to communicate her passion. Her chocolates are a must. And her smile is so heartwarming.

Pierre Koffmann

Why buy another cookery book? It's a

hard question to answer. All I can say is that I have hundreds. One of my most treasured possessions, for example, is a little book by Edouard de Pomiane, illustrated by Toulouse-Lautrec and published at the turn of the last century. I can never resist bookshops and I still haunt them, hoping always to come across, say, a Brillat-Savarin, a rare first edition of Hannah Glasse, or a collection of brilliant ideas by a cook I've never come across before.

This book is largely inspired by the magnificent fresh ingredients to be found on the Isle of Harris. I went there to cook for the season and loved it so much that now I seem likely never to leave this enchanted place. The fish, particularly, is the best and freshest I have ever found, and the sweet lamb and lean venison from the hill would make any cook leap at the chance to do her very best with them. But thanks to modern marketing and communication, most of these ingredients can now be found in supermarkets all over the world.

I have worked for some of the best chefs of our time – particularly Pierre Koffmann and Jean-Christophe Novelli, for whose encouragement I am profoundly grateful. My style is based on classic French tradition, with my own personal twist. Sometimes I literally dream up recipes at night, sometimes I am fired by a sudden idea and experiment until I find what I consider the very best way of putting it into practice.

Although I have usually suggested the ideal way of achieving the desired effect, I do hope that you will improvise and experiment with these recipes. Not everyone can have a flourishing herb garden, or several stock-pots on the go at the same time, and occasionally dried herbs, a bought bouillon or a stock-cube will have to be used. Don't worry. Above all, don't forget that good cooking will generate laughter, friendship and camaraderie. It really should be fun!

I hope that you will find plenty to read and enjoy in this book, and that one day I might see you on a cookery course at Amhuinnsuidhe Castle.

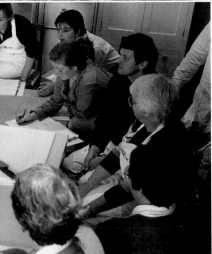

A morning shellfish class at Rosemary's Cookery School.

Shellfish

Mussel and Octopus Spaghetti

Some people are rather squeamish about octopus. Give them this: they'll probably not realise what it is, but when you tell them they'll be converted. There is a theory that the way to soften up an octopus – which does tend to be a tough creature – is to add a wine cork to the court-bouillon as it cooks.

Serves 4

1 kg mussels
500 g octopus
350 g spaghetti
2 shallots, finely chopped
4 cloves garlic, finely chopped
8 tomatoes, skinned, deseeded and chopped
2 tablespoons parsley
150 ml white wine
1 litre court-bouillon (see Basics)
olive oil and extra virgin olive oil
seasoning

Simmer the octopus for an hour in the court-bouillon. While it is cooking, clean the mussels, removing the beards and any barnacles, and cook them in the wine, in a large pan, until they have all opened (discard any that remain stubbornly closed after 5 minutes). Strain them, reserving the wine in which they were cooked and remove half of them from their shells.

Drain and skin the octopus and chop it up into small pieces: add it to the shelled mussels. Now soften the shallots and the garlic in olive oil, stir in the tomatoes and add the reserved wine, letting it simmer for a few minutes until it thickens. Then stir in the octopus and shelled mussels and let the whole thing warm gently for a couple of minutes.

Boil the spaghetti until just soft and strain it. Add the mussels still in their shells to the cooked spaghetti, with some extra virgin olive oil, the parsley and seasoning. Finally stir in the octopus and mussel sauce.

Mussel Soup

Serves 4

2 kg mussels
4 shallots, finely chopped
2 cloves garlic, finely chopped
4 sprigs parsley
zest of one orange
1/2 bottle white wine
60 g butter
1 rounded tablespoon flour
500 ml fish stock (see Basics)
100 ml double cream
1 teaspoon cumin
seasoning
1 tablespoon chopped chives for garnish

Clean the mussels, removing the barnacles and beards. Simmer half the shallots, garlic, parsley and orange zest in the wine for a minute or two then add the mussels and boil them until they are all open. If, after 5 minutes, some of them haven't opened, throw those away. Strain the juice through a fine sieve and reserve it.

Take about 20 of the best looking cooked mussels and reserve them for later. Then shell all the others. Rinse the pan and soften the rest of the shallots in the butter, then add the flour and cumin and cook it gently for a minute before stirring in the vinous mussel-juice and the fish stock. Simmer it gently for about 15 minutes before adding the shelled mussels for the last 5 minutes.

Liquidise the soup and pass it again through a fine sieve, pushing it all through, even if it takes a bit of time. Finally heat it through gently with the rest of the mussels, and serve it sprinkled with chives.

Crab

The shores of Great Britain are surrounded by crabs and the Isle of Harris is no exception. The heavier a crab is, the better. Another good sign, besides weight, is a fine encrustation of barnacles and other knobbly bits: this indicates that the crab hasn't recently lost its shell.

A good deal of folklore surrounds the sexing of fish but in this case the general preference for the male is justified, if for nothing else than for the meatiness of its claws. To find out which you have picked up, turn it over and inspect the back – taking great care as the claws can be vicious if they haven't been secured. If it is a male, it will have a long, narrow tail, folded onto the shell; the female has a broader, slightly heart-shaped tail.

As with lobsters, it is a good idea to put them in the fridge for several hours to become soporific before cooking them in a large pan of rapidly boiling salted water. Most crabs weigh about a kilo and will take about 25 minutes to cook – obviously, allow a little more time for the larger ones.

You'll need plenty of time to prepare them: it is a fiddly business, requiring separate bowls for white meat and brown, a bucket for the rubbish and a large glass of white wine to see you through. But it really is worth it, not only for the sense of achievement when you have finished but because the taste is exquisite.

Start by snapping off all the legs and claws and remove all the white meat from them, using skewers or similar implements. Turn the crab on its side, head downwards, and give it a bash (2) with your fist: this should separate the body from the shell. Next, press your thumb down on the mouth and crack it. The head should come away: discard it along with the 'dead man's fingers' and (3) anything that looks greenish or watery.

Now take all the brown meat from the shell, then take the white meat from the centre of the crab (4) and from the claws (5), scraping it out from all the little nooks and crannies: it is worth doing this properly as this is the sweetest meat. Congratulate yourself: you have finished.

It is wonderful just like this, with a little lemony mayonnaise and some fresh bread – or you could try one of the following recipes.

Crab Soup

If you are happy to prepare the crabs yourself, which does take time, take the meat from the shells, separating brown meat from white and keeping both; you will also need to keep the shells. If this doesn't take your fancy, ask your kind fishmonger to do it for you.

Serves 8–10

2 large cooked crabs
500 g prawns, shell-on (optional)
2³/₄ litre fish stock (see Basics)
¹/₂ bottle dry white wine
1 small bulb fennel, chopped
1 large onion, chopped
1 leek, chopped
1 carrot, chopped
4 cloves garlic, chopped
2 sprigs fresh thyme
a pinch of cayenne papper
250 g tomatoes, quartered
2 tablespoons tomato purée
2 potatoes, chopped
4 tablespoons olive oil
1 tablespoon saffron mayonnaise (see Basics)
seasoning

Using a large pan, soften the fennel, onion, leek, carrot and garlic in 3 tablespoons of the olive oil. Add the crab shells and the wine: bring it to the boil and allow it to simmer for a minute or two. Now add the fish stock and simmer for a further 30 minutes. Strain it into a large bowl, pressing the contents thoroughly so as to extract maximum flavour.

Wipe out the pan and heat the remaining tablespoon of olive oil with the tomatoes and thyme, cooking them together for a moment before adding the purée and cooking for another minute. Add the strained stock, the brown crab meat, the potatoes and the prawns and simmer for a further 10 minutes. Finally, liquidise the soup and rub it through a fine sieve.

Mix the white crab meat with the saffron mayonnaise, season and serve the soup with two teaspoonsful of this mixture floating on top of each bowl.

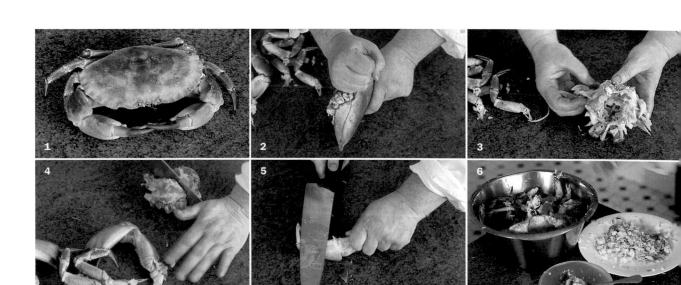

Crab Soufflé

Despite their reputation, soufflés are dead easy to make. The only problem is getting your guests ready to eat them just as soon as you have taken them from the oven. When Lily Macdonald was in charge of the cooking at Morsgail Lodge, Lewis, in the early 1960s, she used her famous cheese soufflé as an extra dinner-bell: 'I'd cook for about 18 in the dining-room and 8 ghillies in the staff-room', she told us 'and they'd stay drinking gin in the hall forever, unless I told them there was a soufflé – then they'd know they had to hurry'. This one makes use of our local crab – but you can flavour the recipe with many other ingredients, exactly as you like, bearing in mind that it is vital that the basic sauce has a strong taste.

Serves 6

60 g butter
60 g plain flour
300 ml milk
300 g prepared white crab meat
1 tablespoon grated Gruyère cheese
3 tablespoons grated Parmesan cheese
10 egg-whites
4 egg-yolks
a good pinch of cayenne pepper
1 teaspoon garam masala
seasoning

You will also need 6 ramekin dishes, well buttered, sprinkled with one tablespoon of the Parmesan and then chilled in the fridge.

Oven 180C/ 350F/ Gas 4

Use the first three ingredients to make a very thick white sauce (see Basics), taking care not to brown the roux. After two minutes of gentle cooking, remove the pan from the heat and stir in both cheeses.

Allow it to cool a little and fold in the crab. Now beat in the egg-yolks, one at a time, and add spices and seasoning. Transfer it to a large bowl.

Whisk the egg-whites until they hold their shape and stir a little into the mixture to slacken it, then fold in the rest. Take care not to be too energetic about this, so as to retain as much air as possible. Spoon the mixture into the cold ramekins and level the surfaces. Run your thumb around the inside edge of each dish to help the souffles rise evenly.

Bake for 10 minutes – check after 8 – and serve instantly.

Crab Risotto

You can vary this dish by adding a few mussels, if you like – in which case, keep them in their shells for maximum dramatic effect – or cooked fresh green peas, in season. Be prepared to be flexible about the liquid: you may need a little more, or a little less. The final result should be creamy.

Serves 6 as a first course, or 4 as a light lunch

400 g white crab meat
250 ml dry white wine
250 g arborio/risotto rice
2 shallots, finely chopped
1 medium leek, finely chopped
1 dessertspoon tarragon
1 dessertspoon chives
115 g butter
600 ml fish stock (see Basics)
150 ml double cream
a good pinch of cayenne pepper
seasoning
1 dessertspoon chervil for garnish

250 g cooked mussels (optional)
150 g fresh peas (optional)

Soften the shallots and the leek in the butter, then turn the rice in the mixture and add the wine. Over a very low heat, allow the rice to absorb the wine, stirring continuously, then gradually add the fish stock, keeping the heat low and waiting until it is nearly dry before each addition.

After about 25 to 30 minutes, when the rice still has a little bite left, fold in the tarragon and chives followed by the crab meat, the cream, cayenne, seasoning and – if you're using them – the cooked mussels and/or peas.

Sprinkle the chervil over the top before serving.

Castellated Crab

Wonderful crabs can be fished from the waters just below the walls of Amhuinnsuidhe Castle. This recipe is one for the cook/architect. It is a bit fiddly to assemble but you can prepare it all up to an hour in advance and it will undoubtedly impress your guests. Of course it is also scrumptious.

Serves 6 as a first course, or 4 as a light lunch

450 g white crab meat
2 ripe avocado pears
6 large ripe tomatoes
1 teaspoon dill
2 tablespoons mayonnaise (see Basics)
seasoning
juice of 2 lemons
1 sprig fresh dill for garnish

You will also need a metal or plastic ring, about 6 cm in diameter (or 8 cm if you think of serving this dish as a light lunch) and 5 cm in height.

Skin the tomatoes and remove the seeds; dice and season them and put them aside. Skin the avocadoes, chop them in horizontal rings and put them into the lemon juice. Mix the crab meat with the dill and mayonnaise and season the mix.

Build each little circular castle from the bottom up, using your ring and compressing the layers as you go. Start with a layer of diced tomato, followed by avocado, followed by one layer of crab. Put more avocado on top of the crab and finish with another layer of tomatoes, topped with a frond of dill. Serve it with some basil oil.

Basil Oil

Basil is particularly good with all tomato dishes. This oil will keep for about three weeks.

Serves 6

150 ml extra virgin olive oil
a good bunch of basil
salt

Liquidise the basil with about one dessertspoon olive oil. Stir in the rest of olive oil and salt and leave it in a bowl for about a day before straining it through muslin (or a tea towel) so that it is clear. Store it in a screw-topped jar.

Lobster

The cold waters of the Sound of Taransay are home to many fine lobsters. Every chef who lives near the sea thinks his or her local lobsters are the best. However they are all wrong. Mine are.

Alive, lobsters are very dark blue-black in colour: when cooked they turn a reddish pink. I tend to prefer the smaller specimens, weighing only about 600 g each, as they are generally the sweetest and most succulent. A local fisherman told me that one of the reasons ours are so sweet is that the rocks in the neighbourhood of the Sound provide plenty of cubby-holes in which they can rest.

The way to sex a lobster is to turn it upside down and check the length of the spikes underneath the tail: the longer ones are male, the shorter female. The only reason for finding out (unless of course you're another lobster) is that some people prefer the taste of the female, though I think there's little to choose between them.

There are many theories about the best way of killing a lobster but at Amhuinnsuidhe, I prefer to send them into a sleepy state first by putting them into the fridge for at least four hours. Then I plunge them into rapidly boiling sea water (or salted water), the lid clapped on again as soon as

possible to retain the heat (I would never boil more than three at a time, as it's important that the temperature rises again very quickly). An alternative way of killing them is to dispatch them briskly with a large, sharp knife.

To clean them, snap off the two large claws, then the legs (1). Stretch the lobster out and slice it in half lengthwise firmly, with a large knife (2). Remove the meat from the claws (3). Identify, remove and discard the stomach-sack from its head, then the intestine – a thin black line running down towards a smaller bag in the tail. Remove any coral you may find and also any dark greenish meat for possible future use: this latter is the liver, or 'tomalley' and turns bright red when cooked. Everything that remains is delicious (4).

There are several lobster recipes in this section, so the only other thing to add here is that the big mistake some people make is to cook them for too long, turning them rubbery. Seven minutes (from boiling point) per 600 g is the maximum time you should give them .

Lobster Salad
with Lime and Tarragon

'A woman should never be seen eating or drinking, unless it be lobster salad and champagne'.
Lord Byron (1788–1824)

So here is a lovely, fresh summer salad, which you might like to use for a special picnic when you can expect to be publicly observed.

Serves 4

4 live lobsters, each weighing 600 g
4 sprigs dill

For the lime mayonnaise:
1 egg-yolk
150 ml sunflower oil
juice of 1^1/$_2$ limes, strained
zest of 1 lime
1 tablespoon fresh tarragon leaves, finely chopped
seasoning

Make the lobsters sleepy by refrigerating them for a couple of hours – four if you can – while you make the mayonnaise (see Basics). Stir in the lime juice and zest and the herbs. Season to taste.

Cook and clean the lobsters as described on page 20. Arrange the meat on a plate, keeping it whole as far as possible and serve it garnished with dill and accompanied by the lime mayonnaise and the following salad.

New Potato and Broad Bean Salad

Serves 4

750 g new potatoes, scraped
180 g young broad beans
^{1}/$_2$ bulb fennel, diced
1 tablespoon mint leaves, cut into strips

For the vinaigrette:
150 ml extra virgin olive oil
juice of 1 lemon, strained
1 tablespoon dill, finely chopped
seasoning

Unless the beans are very tiny, slip the skins off them before cooking them briefly in boiling water. Put the new potatoes into boiling water, with a little salt and a sprig of mint and cook them for 10 minutes or until they are tender.

Drain them and cut them into small cubes. As they cool a little, combine all the ingredients for the vinaigrette in a large bowl, add the warm vegetables and mix everything together.

Lobster with Turbot

I admit that this dish is not cheap. But if you want to push the boat out one day, do give it a try. It is sumptuous.

Serves 4

2 live lobsters, each weighing 600 g
500 g turbot, skinned and filleted
750 ml fish stock (see Basics)
a good bunch of tarragon
a good bunch of parsley
a good bunch of dill
300 ml double cream
60 ml dry vermouth
30 g butter, melted
sprigs of chervil to garnish
salt
4 carrots
4 courgettes

Oven 200C/ 400F/ Gas 6

Make the lobsters sleepy for a couple of hours in the fridge and then plunge them into a large pan of boiling water, clapping the lid on tight and boiling them for 7 minutes. Clean them, discarding the stomach, intestine and liver (see page 21) and reserve the meat.

Next, peel the carrots and courgettes and, with a small paring knife, shape them into little barrels, producing 'turned' vegetables. Boil them (separately) in salted water until just tender, then drain and refresh them.

Heat the fish stock with the bunches of herbs and simmer until reduced by a half. Remove from the heat and allow the herbs to infuse for half an hour.

Strain the sauce, return it to the pan with the cream and reduce again for 5 minutes before stirring in the vermouth – the sauce should still be quite thin. Add salt to taste and set it aside.

Cut the turbot into rectangles, roughly 8 cm x 3 cm, salt them and bake them for 5 minutes on a buttered tray.

Heat the sauce, stir the lobster meat and the turned vegetables into it, then simmer the whole pot gently for a couple of minutes to warm it up. Serve it with the turbot, garnished with chervil. Baby new potatoes go well with this dish.

Above, roasting lobsters. *Opposite page*, choosing lobsters with John.

Roast Lobster Sauternes

This is one of the favourites at Amhuinnsuidhe: everybody seems to love it. It is simple to make, once you understand how the anatomy of the fish works. You can make the whole dish in advance, up to ✱.

Serves 4

4 live lobsters, each weighing 600 g
120 g butter, melted
1 tablespoon chives, chopped
1 tablespoon dill, chopped

For the sauce:
1 shallot, finely chopped
170 ml dry white wine
300 ml double cream
170 ml Sauternes
salt

Oven 220C/ 425F/ Gas 7

Cook the lobsters and allow them to cool.

Remove the two large claws, then the legs. Cut the lobsters in half lengthwise, firmly, with a large knife – you want to keep the shell intact (see illustration 4 on page 21). Identify, remove and discard the stomach-sack. Do the same with the tiny, black thread-like intestine and then find the greenish meat (the tomalley) near the head and reserve it for future use in pasta or sauces. Take all the meat out of the claws and pack it into the clean head.

Now make the sauce. Simmer the shallot with the white wine and reduce it to one third. Add the cream and reduce it again, by half, then stir in the Sauternes and some salt. ✱

Brush the surface of the lobsters with the melted butter and sprinkle them with salt. Roast them for 10 minutes. Reheat the sauce and serve with the fish, sprinkled with fresh herbs.

Scallops

These wonderful molluscs are very plentiful in the Western Isles, readily available to us at our beck and call. We buy them alive, for maximum freshness, so that they are often still actually pulsating as they are shelled: this sometimes alarms the guests on our courses. We usually refer to them as scallops but many Hebridean people call them clams, which confused me when I first arrived.

I only buy scallops from divers who have gathered them by hand: this is not merely to do with the quality of the scallops themselves, but because divers can find them in places where dredgers cannot reach. Also, the dredgers do considerable harm to the ecology of the seabed. Ours tend to be larger than those found in shops – I weighed one, out of interest, whose meat alone weighed 150 g.

In the sea, a scallop propels itself about by skilful snapping of the shells: it's very charming to watch. However, the shells are clamped tight shut when you come to try and cook them and have to opened with great care.

Hold the scallop, flat side up – you might like to protect your hands with a thick cloth. Put the point of a small, strong knife into the gap near the hinge and twist it sharply to open it (1). Then take a longer-bladed knife and slide it right across, just inside the flatter shell, severing the connecting muscle: this automatically opens the whole thing up. Scoop it from the other half, with a similar action, keeping the contents intact (2). On a board, cut off the frill (which is really the scallop's 50 eyes) and keep it for sauces. Discard everything else except the pink roe and the white meat. Keep these covered, on a cloth in the fridge for as little time as possible.

As with so many fish, scallops must never be overcooked – they need the briefest time imaginable and are even perfectly delicious eaten raw, finely sliced and dressed with olive oil, pepper and lemon juice.

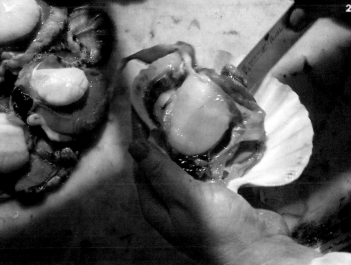

Seared Scallops
with Rocket and Red Pepper Salsa

Really fresh scallops take well to very rapid searing. In this case, the scallops are turned in oil before cooking: it is important not to shift them about in the pan but just to turn them once. If you don't like red peppers, this recipe is just as good if you use a little extra virgin olive oil and balsamic vinegar as a dressing.

Serves 4 as a first course

12 fresh scallops, shelled and cleaned
1 bunch of rocket, prepared

For the red pepper salsa:
2 large red peppers
1 large tomato
1/2 small fresh red chilli, deseeded and very finely chopped
olive oil
1 teaspoon lemon juice
1 teaspoon white wine vinegar
1/2 teaspoon caster sugar
salt

Oven 220C/ 425F/ Gas 7

Roast the peppers with a little olive oil for 25 to 30 minutes, turning them once. Cool them a little, plunge them into cold water, remove the skins and seeds and chop them very finely.

Skin, deseed and chop the tomato, equally small, mixing it with the peppers, sugar, chilli, a good pinch of salt, the vinegar and one tablespoon of olive oil.

Salt the scallops and turn them in cold olive oil. Heat a dry frying pan and sear the scallops rapidly, turning them only once.

Toss the rocket with the lemon juice and a tablespoonful of olive oil. Put a little pile of rocket in the middle of each plate and surround it with scallops and a spoonful of the red pepper salsa.

Mousseline of Scallops

This is a pretty first course, light and delicate.

Serves 4

250 g fresh scallops, with no coral
1 egg-white
2 large carrots
275 ml double cream
1 teaspoon salt
a pinch of cayenne pepper
250 g fresh spinach
50 g butter, and a little more for buttering
   the moulds

For the sauce:
250 ml fish stock (see Basics)
a good handful of mixed fresh herbs – dill,
   tarragon, parsley, coriander, in whatever
   combination is available
4 tablespoons dry white wine
1 shallot, finely chopped
150 ml double cream
240 g cold butter, cut into small cubes

You will also need 4 little moulds – ideally,
90–100 ml dariole moulds, but small ramekins
will do – generously buttered.

Oven 190C/ 375F/ Gas 5

Using a mandolin or a potato-peeler, slice the
carrot lengthwise into very thin, broad strips.
Blanch them for 2 minutes, then refresh and dry
them on kitchen paper. Use them to line the
moulds, leaving enough overlap to fold over
the top.

Put the scallops into a food-processor and
process until smooth. Add the egg-white, cayenne
and salt. Using the 'pulse' button, add the cream,
taking care not to curdle it by over-mixing. Pass
it through a sieve, one spoonful at a time then
spoon the mixture into the moulds, smoothing
the surface. Fold the slices of carrot over the
top. Wrap each in buttered tinfoil and bake in a
bain-marie for 20 minutes.

While it cooks, prepare the sauce: put the stock
with the herbs in a saucepan and bring it to the
boil. Simmer until it is reduced to about a third,
then strain it into a jug. Put the chopped shallot
into the saucepan, add the wine and boil it, until
the liquid has evaporated to about a tablespoonful.
Over a low heat, beat in the butter thoroughly,
little by little, followed by the cream and finally the
reduced stock from the jug. Season to taste.

Wash and drain the spinach; turn it gently in the
melted butter over a low heat until it wilts, then
strain it.

Turn each mousseline onto a bed of spinach and
serve warm, surrounded by the sauce.

Scallops in a Paper Bag
with Egg Noodle and Ginger

Serves 4 as a first course

8 large scallops
75 g fine egg noodles
2 shallots, finely chopped
100 g carrots, cut into fine julienne strips
3 cm root ginger, cut into fine julienne strips
4 spring onions, cut into fine julienne strips
1 tablespoon chopped basil
100 ml fish stock (see Basics)
140 ml double cream
60 g butter
olive oil
seasoning

You will also need 4 sheets of parchment paper, 25 cm x 38 cm (greaseproof will do, but it is not quite as good).

Oven 220C/ 425F/ Gas 7

Prepare the scallops (see page 27), reserving the juice and frills, then slice them in half horizontally, adding a little olive oil. Boil the noodles until almost cooked.

Soften the shallots in the butter with the carrots, ginger and seasoning and cook them gently for 3 minutes. Take them out and reserve them, leaving any juices in the pan – to which you now add the juice and frills from the scallops, and the fish stock. Bring it to the boil and reduce it for a minute before adding the cream. Strain it and pass it through a fine sieve. Fold the basil into the noodles and season them, adding just a little of the sauce to slacken the texture slightly.

Sear the scallops very rapidly in a dry pan. Make paper parcels: using one sheet per person, fold the papers in half, widthways, to give them a crease, and open them up again. Pile up tiny quantities of noodles, vegetables, and 4 slices of scallop per person on one side of the fold (1). Pour some sauce over the whole (2). Fold the paper over the top and crimp it, as in a Cornish pasty (3). Cook them for 5 minutes. Snip a hole in the top of each bag to let the steam escape.

Langoustines are sometimes called Dublin Bay prawns, but neither is an appropriate name for a shellfish so common around the Hebrides. Perhaps it is for this reason that the islanders call them simply prawns.

There is a long-standing prejudice against eating such shellfish in the islands. It is quite possible that it dates from the time of the Clearances, when people who stayed on the island were so destitute that shellfish were their only diet. They have become an atavistic symbol of utter, hopeless destitution. On the other hand, they are still there to be fished, and bringing them ashore provides a welcome and comparatively profitable living for the fishermen.

Most of the langoustines here are caught by the fleet which goes out from Rodel harbour. There are about 20 boats and they travel daily 12 miles to the south, where a hundred pots, or creels, are strung out on a line, each baited with half a herring. There's a buoy at each end, so that the fishermen can lift the whole line at once to empty the pots. They always throw the smallest back, to give them – as one of them, Donald Norman Maclean, says – 'a fighting chance'.

I buy them in 3 sizes, the largest being almost as big as a small lobster. They are fiendish creatures to handle, being all spikes and lashing claws. I always cool them off in the fridge for several hours to lessen the peril to my hands.

It is fine to cook them briefly, whole, in boiling water for 5 minutes and serve them with garlic butter, but several of my recipes require you to take them apart raw. It's not difficult. Take the pincers off first and then the head, scooping out and discarding the inside and reserving the shell for stock. Take the rest of the shell off the tail – take care, it can be quite sharp – and add it to the stock-pot. Use the meat as described in the following recipes.

Seafood Feuilletés

This little jewel-box of light, crispy pastry can be filled with any treasures from the sea. Here I use langoustines and scallops. If you use frozen pastry it works but, if you go to the trouble of making your own, it is magnificent. It can be prepared a few hours in advance, up to the ✻.

Serves 4 as a generous first course

500 g puff pastry (see Basics)
8 large langoustines or Dublin Bay prawns, shelled
8 large scallops, shelled, washed and cleaned
450 g fresh spinach, washed and prepared
30 g butter
3 tablespoons extra virgin olive oil
1 egg-yolk, lightly beaten
1 tablespoon chives, chopped
a handful of fresh tarragon leaves

For the sauce:
1 shallot, chopped
230 ml fish stock (see Basics)
115 ml dry vermouth
2 pieces of preserved stem ginger in syrup,
    chopped, syrup reserved
a good pinch of saffron
200 ml double cream
seasoning

Oven 200C/ 400F/ Gas 6

Roll out the pastry to 1 cm thickness then cut it into 4 rectangles. Using a sharp knife, score the pastry 1 cm inside the edge, like a picture frame, taking care not to cut it all the way through. Put the squares onto a baking tray and brush them with egg-yolk, making sure you don't go over the edges or the pastry will not rise evenly. Bake for 15 minutes, until golden brown.

While it is still hot, remove the inner squares (which are going to be the lids) and discard the stodgy insides, so that you have 4 clean boxes. ✻

Blanch and refresh the spinach. Drain it and squeeze all the water from it. Make the sauce by softening the shallot in the vermouth and reducing it, before adding the fish stock and reducing it again, to a third. Add the ginger, the saffron and the cream and simmer for two minutes. Season and add a little ginger syrup, to taste. Keep it warm.

To finish the dish, make sure the scallops are dry, then slice them in half horizontally and turn them, with the langoustines, in the olive oil and a pinch of salt. Sear them quickly on both sides in a very hot, dry frying pan. Pop the pastry cases in the oven for a minute if you need to reheat them.

Turn the spinach in the butter over a gentle heat and assemble the feuilletés by putting a spoonful of spinach in the bottom of each pastry-box and filling it with shellfish and some sauce. Sprinkle with chives and tarragon and put the lid on top.

Langoustine Salad
with Orange and Olive Oil Dressing

Squat lobsters or 'squatties' as we call them, are becoming increasingly available in supermarkets. They are as tasty as their larger cousins and can be used in their place if you like. This simple salad is served with a delicious orange-flavoured cold dressing, and with tossed mixed herbs. It can be prepared up to the ✶ as much as a day before.

Serves 4

about 20 langoustines or 40 squat lobsters, shelled
mixed herb and salad leaves
2 tomatoes, skinned, deseeded and diced
1 tablespoon chives, chopped
1 tablespoon vinaigrette (see Basics)
olive oil
seasoning

For the dressing:
3 shallots, finely chopped
4 cloves garlic, finely chopped
75 ml white wine vinegar
175 ml olive oil
150 ml water
zest and juice of 2 oranges
1/2 red chilli, finely diced
some sprigs of oregano, parsley, basil
2 bay leaves
1 teaspoon caster sugar

Salt the langoustines and leave them to stand. Make the dressing by combining all the ingredients in a small pan, bringing it to the boil and allowing it to simmer and thicken slightly for 20 minutes before cooling and straining it through a fine sieve.

Heat some olive oil in a frying pan and cook the langoustines gently for 30 seconds on each side turning them only once. Cool them on kitchen paper to remove excess oil, then toss them in the dressing and chill them until required. ✶

Toss the mixed herbs with the vinaigrette and serve the langoustines with the dressing spooned over them, arranged around a little pile of herb salad, the whole garnished with the chives and tomatoes.

Squat lobsters, or 'squatties'.

Langoustine Ravioli
with a Red Pepper Sauce

This is one of my very favourite dishes. It really isn't too difficult to make and the wonderful thing about it is that you can prepare it well in advance and leave it sitting in your fridge until you're ready to use it.

Serves 4 as a first course

1 portion pasta (see Basics)
24 langoustines (or Dublin Bay prawns)
2 egg-yolks, lightly beaten
1 tablespoon finely chopped chives for garnish
a bunch of chervil for garnish

For the marinade:
1 rasher bacon, finely diced
2 small shallots, finely diced
1 small clove garlic, finely diced
1 teaspoon fresh root ginger, finely diced
20 g butter

For the sauce:
4 medium red peppers
200 ml double cream
30 g butter
3 tablespoons olive oil

Oven 220C/ 425F/ Gas 7

Remove the heads and shells from the langoustines – take great care as they can be sharp. Combine the marinade ingredients in a small frying pan and allow them to cook very gently, until all the flavours have intermingled. Transfer it to a large bowl and turn the prepared langoustines in it. Allow it to cool.

Put two langoustines together at 8 cm intervals along each ribbon of pasta (1), then brush outside the fish and along the edges with egg-yolk. Cover the whole thing with a second ribbon and press down to make ravioli squares (2), before cutting them apart into individual parcels. Pinch the edges together, using floured fingers. Put the parcels, uncovered, into the fridge while you make the sauce.

Roll the peppers in the olive oil then roast them for 25–30 minutes. Remove them from the oven, plunge them into cold water and slip them out of their skins. Chop them on a board, discarding the seeds and the core, and puree them in a liquidiser. Then bring them to simmering point in a small pan, with the cream. Pass the mixture through a fine sieve and keep it warm.

Cook the ravioli for 4 minutes in plenty of boiling salted water, drain it thoroughly until all the water has run out and finish the sauce, just before serving, by whisking in the butter. Finally, sprinkle the chopped chives and sprigs of chervil on top of the ravioli.

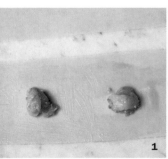

Fish

Haddock Tapenade

This is an inexpensive and unusual dish, easy to prepare in advance and very tasty. You can cook the fish as separate fillets or in an open gratin dish, with the cheese-mixture covering the whole surface. I like to use Isle of Mull cheese but a good quality white cheddar will do.

Serves 8 as a first course, or 4 as a main course

4 fresh haddock fillets, each weighing 180–200 g
4 teaspoons tapenade (see Basics)

For the topping:
25 g butter
75 g grated cheddar cheese
50 g full-fat soft cream cheese
1 egg-yolk
2 egg-whites
a pinch of paprika

Oven 200C/ 400F/ Gas 6

Gently melt the butter and cheddar together, stirring very vigorously, then let the mixture cool in the pan. When it is nearly cold, add the cream cheese, stirring it again, thoroughly, followed by the egg-yolk. Add the paprika. Whisk the egg-whites until firm and fold them gently into the cheese-mixture. Put the whole thing into the fridge for a little while, up to half an hour.

Spread a thin layer of tapenade onto each haddock fillet, followed by a layer of the cheese mixture. Bake them, uncovered, in a buttered baking dish for 10 to 12 minutes. Neaten the edges, if you like, and serve it on a bed of ratatouille.

Ratatouille

This wonderfully versatile dish, making use of the abundance of late summer vegetables, is as good cold as hot. You should chop the vegetables very small if you intend to use the ratatouille as part of this haddock recipe, but more coarsely should you want it as an extra vegetable dish with, say, roast lamb.

1 medium onion, chopped
2 cloves garlic, crushed
500 g tomatoes, skinned, deseeded and chopped
1 teaspoon caster sugar
2 courgettes, cubed
1 red pepper, deseeded and cubed
1 aubergine, diced
plenty of extra virgin olive oil
fresh basil

Soften the garlic and onion in the oil, add the tomatoes, sugar, salt and pepper and cook for 5 minutes. Remove them from the pan and set them aside. Wipe the pan with paper, add some more oil and cook the courgettes in the same way, adding them to the tomatoes (they will take a little less time).

Do the same to the other vegetables. Season to taste. Just before serving stir in some basil. It can happily be reheated.

Braised Halibut
with a Rich Red Wine Sauce

I dreamed this up in the early hours of the morning. It may seem controversial to use red wine with fish, but it works like my dream. Halibut is a dry fish which takes well to this kind of treatment, but be sure not to overcook it. You should also take care not to allow the wine to colour the whole fish: it should leave a pink frill around the edge.

Serves 4

4 halibut fillets, skinned, each weighing about 180g
125 ml red wine
2 medium aubergines
olive oil
seasoning
sage leaves for garnish

For the sauce:
280 ml red wine
280 ml fish stock (see Basics)
1 tablespoon redcurrant jelly
60 g butter

For the potatoes:
4 large potatoes
90 g butter
100 ml warm milk
2 sage leaves, chopped
seasoning

Oven 200C/ 400F/ Gas 6

Slice aubergines into 3 mm rounds and bake them in olive oil until soft and golden (not crisp). Drain them on kitchen paper. Prepare the fish by neatening the edges and ensuring that all bones are removed.

Peel and boil the potatoes, then sieve them and beat in the butter and the milk, followed by the sage and seasoning. Keep them warm.

Make the sauce by putting the red wine and jelly in a small pan and reducing it by half. Add the fish stock and leave it simmering until it is again reduced by half.

Cook the fish like this: pour the 125 ml red wine into a shallow ovenproof dish and put the fish fillets on top. Cover the dish with foil and braise it in the oven for 8 minutes, then remove it and leave it to rest, still covered, for 5 minutes.

Deep-fry the remaining sage leaves until crisp (it will take about 30 seconds) and save them for decoration, then finish the sauce by adding the butter to the pan over a low heat, whisking it all the time.

To serve, arrange slices of aubergine in a fan shape. Put a spoonful of potato on top, surmounted by the fish. Decorate it with the crisp sage and surround it with the sauce – the rest of the sauce can be served in a jug.

Halibut with Flageolet Beans

This is a hearty and sustaining dish but it takes time to prepare. You have to start the day before, as the beans need to be soaked in cold water overnight. In some recipes, tinned flageolets can be used instead of the dried variety but in this dish they would not produce quite such a delicious flavour.

Serves 4

4 halibut fillets, skinned, each weighing
about 170–180 g
1 litre fish stock (see Basics)
200 g dried flageolet beans, soaked overnight
in cold water
1 onion, diced
2 cloves garlic, diced
4 tomatoes, skinned, deseeded and roughly
chopped
2 bay leaves
2 medium carrots, sliced into rounds
2 tablespoons olive oil (and a little more for
the fish)
2 tablespoons fresh coriander, chopped, and
4 sprigs, for decoration
4 large sprigs parsley
seasoning

Oven 200C/ 400F/ Gas 6

Using a large pan, soften the onion and garlic in oil, then add the tomatoes, bay leaves, parsley and stir the mixture together for a minute or two, over a low heat. Drain the beans and add them to the pan, then cover them with fish stock.

Allow the pan to simmer gently for about an hour, topping it up with stock from time to time – it should never become dry. Add the carrots and cook for a further half-hour, testing the beans occasionally. When they are tender, fold in the fresh coriander.

During the last half-hour, after you've added the carrots, cook the fish. Sear it on all sides in hot oil, then bake it, uncovered, in an ovenproof dish for 7 minutes.

Serve the fish on a bed of beans, with a sprig of coriander.

Filleting halibut.

Herrings in Pinhead Oatmeal

Though I had never eaten this dish before
I came to Harris, I now love it – especially for
breakfast. But it makes a good supper, too,
when accompanied by a plain green salad and
new potatoes. Because I am greedy, I have
allowed two herrings per person, but one might
well be enough for a more modest appetite.
If you have trouble finding pinhead oatmeal,
try a good health-food shop.

Serves 4

8 herrings, boned and flattened
250 g pinhead oatmeal
1 tablespoon butter
1 tablespoon olive oil
1 lemon

Spread the oatmeal onto a plate and put the
herrings into it, patting the meal into the surface
of the fish on both sides. Melt the butter and
oil together in a pan and fry the fish on a low
heat for 2 minutes on each side. Serve with a
squeeze of lemon.

Herrings with Couscous

From time immemorial the people of Harris have lived on herrings. Before coming here I had never used them much in cooking, but within weeks of my arrival I was converted. The germ of the idea for this recipe came from a dish I first came across at the Tante Claire restaurant: in that case, the fish was red mullet.

Serves 6 as a first course, or 4 as a light lunch

6 fresh herrings, boned and cut in half
extra virgin olive oil

For the marinade:
6 tablespoons dark soy sauce
1 dessertspoon syrup from a jar of stem ginger
1 dessertspoon sherry

For the couscous:
150 g couscous
200 ml boiling fish stock (see Basics)
100 ml extra virgin olive oil
2 cm grated root ginger
1 red pepper, skinned, deseeded and finely diced
1 tablespoon chives, chopped
1 tablespoon coriander, chopped
seasoning

You will also need a metal or plastic ring, about 6 cm in diameter and 5 cm in height.

Mix the marinade ingredients together and steep the herrings in it for at least an hour. Mix all the couscous ingredients together thoroughly, stirring the mixture frequently.

Take the fish out of the marinade and fry it quickly on both sides in hot oil. Shape the couscous into circles with the ring-mould, and press it down. Run a sharp knife around the inside of the ring to lift it off and arrange the fish on top.

Hamish Taylor's salt herrings.

Turbot with Sole Mousse

Turbot is a wonderful, smooth fish which needs very little cooking, but this dish works equally well with other fish, John Dory for example. If you want to push the boat out, garnish it with caviar.

Serves 4

4 turbot fillets, skinned, each weighing about 180 g
170 ml fish stock (see Basics)
60 g butter, melted
half a cucumber
seasoning

For the mousse:
1 sole fillet, skinned weight about 150 g
150 ml double cream
1 egg-white
1 dessertspoon dry vermouth

For the sauce:
100 ml dry white wine
300 ml fish stock (see Basics)
1 shallot, finely chopped
190 ml double cream
75 ml Pernod
salt
a few sprigs parsley, chervil and dill

Oven 200C/ 400F/ Gas 6

Prepare the mousse: puree the sole in a food-processor until smooth. Add the egg-white, vermouth and a little salt and pepper. Switch on again for 5 seconds. Using the 'pulse' button, add the cream slowly, taking care not to overdo it and cause curdling.

Pass the mousse through a sieve, a little at a time, and refrigerate it for at least 2 hours. Put the turbot fillets on a baking tray. Spread the mousse mixture evenly over each of them. Peel the cucumber and slice it paper-thin, then arrange the slices like scales over the fish. Pour the melted butter over the top and bake it for 10 minutes – it may take a little longer.

Meanwhile, make the sauce. Reduce the wine, with the shallot, to about one third. Add the stock and the herbs and reduce, again to about a third. Add the cream and continue reducing for about 5 minutes. Finally, stir in the Pernod and check the seasoning. This is delicious served on a bed of braised fennel.

Braised Fennel

1 large bulb of fennel
60 g butter
salt and pepper

Remove the outer leaves from the fennel and cut it into strips lengthwise, following the grain. Simmer in boiling water for 2 or 3 minutes. Drain and refresh. Turn the fennel in melted butter over a medium heat until warmed through and season it.

Roast Saffron Monkfish
with Herb Risotto

There is a lot of water in monkfish, so it is better to buy a little more than you think you might need. Saffron is a powerful (and expensive) spice so use it with discretion.

Serves 4

4 monkfish tails, skinned and filletted, each
  weighing about 180 g
1/2 teaspoon turmeric
350 ml dry white wine
a good pinch of saffron

For the risotto:
250 g arborio/risotto rice
2 shallots, finely chopped
1 medium leek, finely chopped
1 dessertspoon parsley, chopped
1 dessertspoon coriander, chopped
1 tablespoon chives, chopped
115 g butter
500 ml fish stock (see Basics)
55 g grated Parmesan cheese
4 tablespoons double cream
seasoning

Oven 200C/ 400F/ Gas 6

Reduce the wine with the saffron and turmeric over a brisk heat, for 2 minutes, then leave it to cool and infuse for half an hour. Dunk the fish in the saffron-wine, turning it until each whole piece is bright yellow. Leave the fish in the wine for a further half-hour, while you start the risotto.

Melt the butter in a broad, shallow pan (a cast-iron skillet is ideal). Soften the shallots and leek, then add the rice, turning it gently. Drain the fish and add the saffron-wine to the rice-mixture. Cook gently while the rice absorbs the liquid, stirring it all the time. As it begins to dry out, add the stock, little by little, still stirring – you may find that you need a little more than 500 ml. After about half an hour, the rice should be just tender and the liquid absorbed. Finally, fold in the cream, the herbs and the Parmesan, so that it becomes almost like a sauce.

Make sure that the fish is dry, then sear it in hot oil before roasting it in the oven for 7 minutes. Allow it to rest on a grid so that the juices run out. Slice the fish with a sharp knife and serve it over a bed of risotto.

Monkfish with Ink Fettuccine
and a Caper and Rosemary Sauce

The amount of pasta you use depends on how greedy your friends are. The minimum is about 35–40 g per person, but this recipe uses more, and will provide a substantial lunch dish. The sauce is strongly flavoured and very tasty and the colours are pleasingly dramatic.

Serves 4

**4 monkfish tails, skinned and filletted, each
  weighing about 180 g**
250 g ink fettucine
4 slices smoked streaky bacon, chopped small
4 large sprigs rosemary
1 rounded tablespoon capers
100 ml dry white wine
300 ml fish stock (see Basics)
200 ml double cream
2 tomatoes, skinned, deseeded and diced
2 tablespoons butter
3 tablespoons olive oil
60 g clarified butter (see Basics)
seasoning

Oven 200C/ 400F/ Gas 6

Fry the bacon in a tablespoon of olive oil, remove it and keep it for the sauce. Wipe the pan with kitchen paper then pour in the wine and reduce it by half. Add the stock to the reduced wine and reduce the whole again by half. Then add the cream and reduce yet again (yes!), to about one third. Stir in the bacon, rosemary, capers and tomatoes and set it aside.

Cook the pasta in plenty of boiling salted water, drain it and toss it in the butter and the rest of the olive oil. Meanwhile, sear the monkfish in the clarified butter then roast it for 8 minutes. Reheat the sauce and serve.

Sole Amhuinnsuidhe

This is our variant of a classic and spectacular dish, making elegant use of the fine fresh fish we enjoy in the Hebrides. I have used squat lobsters, the delicious little crustaceans that abound here, but prawns are nearly as good. You can also use lemon sole, or plaice, instead of Dover sole. The first part is a little fiddly, but the end result is well worth it. Do be careful when sieving the mousse: if you do too much at a time the cream might curdle. It can be prepared well in advance up to the *.

Serves 4

4 small, plump Dover soles
38 prawns or squat lobsters, cooked
220 g salmon fillet, skinned and boned
300 ml double cream
1 egg-white
1 teaspoon salt
60 g butter

For the sauce:
2 tablespoons wine vinegar
2 tablespoons white wine
140 g butter
180 ml double cream
2 tablespoons dry vermouth
1 tablespoon chopped chives for garnish

Remove the head of each fish, and fillet it by cutting through the skin to the spine, then easing the fish off the bone with a very sharp knife either side of the backbone. Turn it over and do the same the other side. With scissors, sever the bone at tail and remove it, making sure that the tail stays attached to the fillets to keep the whole thing together. Trim the smaller bones off the sides of the fish, leaving just a little frill of bone to keep the shape. Arrange the filleted fish, dark side up, on buttered foil on a baking tray, sprinkle it with salt inside and prepare the mousse.

Put the salmon into a food-processor and process it for a minute. Add the egg-white, then, using the 'pulse' button, gently mix in the cream and salt. Sieve it, a little at a time into a clean bowl and chill it thoroughly for an hour in the fridge.

Spoon the mousse (I often use a piping-bag with a broad nozzle for this) into the cavity of each fish (1) and arrange the prawns or squat lobsters along the top (2). Trickle melted butter over the top and cover the whole thing in foil. *

Bake for 20 minutes (check after 15 – the mousse should be firm to the touch).

Meanwhile, make the sauce by reducing the wine and vinegar over a brisk heat until only about one tablespoonful is left. Whisk in the butter, little by little, then stir in the cream and the vermouth and check the seasoning. When the fish is ready, allow it to rest for a minute or two and then lift the skin off the top, and discard it, along with the tail.

Pour the sauce over the fish and sprinkle with chives. This is very good served with tagliatelle, sprinkled with fresh tarragon leaves.

Oriental Sole

This is faintly reminiscent of a classic dish, but where Escoffier might have used cream, these ingredients produce a more aromatic taste. You may think that there will be too much sauce, but Bridget, manager of Amhuinnsuidhe, can never get enough of it! If you only have lemon sole, or plaice, it works just as well.

Serves 4 as a first course

**8 fillets of Dover sole, skinned, each weighing
  130 g, halved lengthwise**
**24 large leaves from a Cos lettuce, hard, white
  central spines removed**
1 shallot, finely diced
250 g shitake mushrooms, finely diced
30 g butter
2 medium carrots, cut into fine julienne strips
3 medium leeks, cut into very fine julienne strips
280 ml fish stock (see Basics)
seasoning

For the sauce:
150 ml extra virgin olive oil
150 ml sunflower oil
150 ml dark soy sauce
2 teaspoons chopped root ginger
3 teaspoons runny honey

Oven 200C/ 400F/ Gas 6

Make the sauce by combining all the ingredients in a bowl. Soften the shallot in the butter and add the mushrooms, cooking them together for 2 minutes before straining them. Blanch one leek with the carrots, strain and refresh them and use them to cover the base of a buttered ovenproof dish.

Blanch the lettuce very briefly, 4 leaves at a time, removing it with a slotted spoon to a cake rack to drain thoroughly. Arrange 3 leaves in a star shape, with a spoonful of mushrooms and shallot in the middle. Arrange 2 fillets of fish folded on top of it all (see below) and make a little parcel by bringing the lettuce leaves up from underneath. As you finish each parcel, turn it upside down so that it keeps its shape and arrange them all on top of the vegetables brushing a little melted butter over the top.

Pour the fish stock into the dish and bake, covered with tinfoil, for about 25 minutes – check for firmness after 20. Toss the rest of the leeks in a little plain flour and deep fry them until crisp. Serve a handful of these leeks on top of each fish. Finally pour the sauce around or over.

Sole with Spinach Tortellini

This is a light and tasty dish but it does take time to prepare. You'll need a round cutter about 8 cm in diameter. If you like, you can assemble the whole thing a few hours in advance, up to the ∗ and store the tortellini, well spaced, on a floured tray in the fridge.

Serves 4

4 fillets of sole, skinned, each weighing about 180 g
1/2 pasta recipe (see Basics)
250 g fresh spinach, washed
4 spring onions, finely chopped
a pinch of chilli powder
1 egg-yolk
1 tablespoon mascarpone cheese
30 g butter

For the sauce:
125 g whole, raw prawns
400 ml fish stock (see Basics)
1 teaspoon tomato purée
2 dessertspoons dry sherry
200 ml double cream
seasoning

Oven 200C/ 400F/ Gas 6

Start with the pasta: prepare it as in Basics up to the ∗, wrap and refrigerate it. Then deal with the spinach: soften the onions in the butter, add the spinach, chilli powder and seasoning to taste, cook for 3 minutes, drain it thoroughly and allow it to cool. Put the mixture into a food-processor, add the cheese and one egg-yolk and process it very briefly. Leave to cool.

Now make the sauce: peel the prawns and reserve them. Put together the heads, shells, tomato purée and the fish stock in a saucepan; bring it to the boil and reduce it by half. Using a potato-masher, smash up all the prawn shells so as to release the maximum flavour, then pass the stock through a sieve. Return the stock to the pan, add the cream and simmer for a couple of minutes. Add the peeled prawns and bring the sauce back to the boil for a minute then liquidise it and sieve it again. Finally return it once more to the pan, add the sherry and warm it through, taking care that it doesn't boil. Set it aside until you are ready to eat.

To make the tortellini, roll out the pasta (again, refer to Basics) and cut it into rounds on a floured surface. Brush the edges with beaten egg-yolk and put half a teaspoon of the spinach mixture in the middle. Fold each into a half moon, bring up the points and twist them together, twice. ∗

Just before you want to eat, bake the fish, covered with foil, on a buttered dish for 3 to 4 minutes. Gently warm the sauce and bring a large pan of salted water to the boil. Cook the pasta for 2 minutes and drain it. To serve this dish, pour some sauce onto each plate then some tortellini, and top it all with the fish.

Graciously acknowledge the applause.

Seafood Tempura
with Pickled Cucumber

This recipe is inspired by Japanese food, which tends to have a wonderful clean taste: this method of cooking makes the most of our super-fresh fish. It has to be deep-fried at the last minute.

Serves 4 as a first course

8 large prawns, shelled
4 large scallops, shelled and dry
12 mussels, cleaned, cooked and shelled
   (see Mussel and Octopus Spaghetti page 12)
sunflower oil
2 courgettes, cut into fine julienne strips
1 aubergine, cut into four fan-shapes
1 piece Nori seaweed
flour for dredging
1 lime

For the batter:
2 egg-yolks
170 ml water
125 g plain flour
1 egg-white
seasoning

For the pickled cucumber:
1 cucumber
1 teaspoon salt
25 ml white wine vinegar
1 tablespoon caster sugar

Start by pickling the cucumber. Peel it and cut it into very, very fine slices. Put it into a colander with the salt, then leave it to drain for about an hour. Finally mix in the vinegar and the sugar.

Now make the batter by beating the egg-yolks and water into the flour, little by little. Then whisk the egg white and fold it into the mixture. Season.

Make 4 bundles of courgette-sticks, wrapped with a strip of piece of Nori. Dredge each bundle in flour and shake off the excess.

Dip the prawns in the batter and deep fry them briskly in hot oil. Do the same with the rest of the fish and the mussels, standing them on kitchen paper afterwards, to absorb any excess oil. Finally, deep fry the aubergine fans and the courgette bundles. Serve the dish garnished with the cucumber and a wedge of fresh lime.

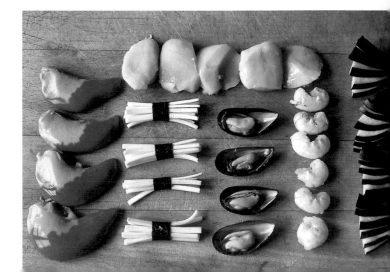

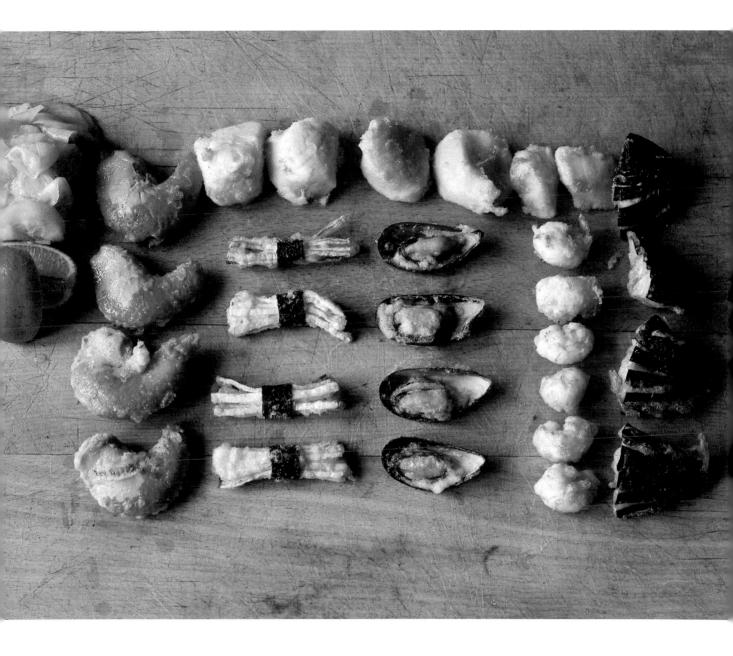

Hebridean Fish Pie

Here is my version of a classic and magnificent dish, warming and comforting, which makes use of the wide variety of fish living in the clear, unpolluted waters around our island. It doesn't really matter which fish you use, but the more variety the better. There is a lot of it: you can use it all at once for a convivial supper party or halve it if there are fewer of you.

Serves 8–10

2^1/$_2$ kg mixed, filleted fish – turbot, haddock, prawns, scallops, salmon, cod, plaice etc.
1 kg mussels
300 ml dry white wine
1 shallot, chopped
1 litre milk
180 g butter
180 g flour
seasoning

For the topping:
1^1/$_2$ kg potatoes, peeled
2 dessertspoons chives, chopped
150 g butter
150 ml milk
1 dessertspoon grated Parmesan cheese
2 beaten eggs

Oven 220C/ 425F/ Gas 7

Clean the mussels, removing barnacles and beards. Bring the wine and shallot to the boil in a large pan and steam the cleaned mussels in it for 15 minutes, until they are all open – as usual, discard any that fail to open after 5 minutes. Strain them through a fine sieve into a large jug and reserve the liquid.

Put all the rest of the fish (except the prawns) into an ovenproof dish and cover it with the milk. Bake for 15 minutes until just cooked. Allow it to cool, then strain off the milk and reserve it with the wine. Carefully remove the skin and any remaining bones from the fish, keeping it in large chunks.

Make a white sauce (see Basics) with the juices in the jug and any more that may have run from the fish. Use plenty of seasoning.

Arrange the cooked fish, the mussels (in their shells or out of them, as you like) and the prawns in a very large ovenproof dish (or two smaller ones). Pour on the sauce, turning the pieces of fish so that they are all covered and allow it all to cool down while you boil and mash the potatoes in the usual way.

Finally mix the chives and Parmesan into the potatoes and spread them over the top of the fish. Score the top with a fork and pour the eggs over the top. Bake for 30–40 minutes.

Smoked Haddock Lasagne

If you can get hold of some dulse (seaweed) for this, use it instead of the coriander for a real taste of the sea, but remember to soak it first. Either vegetable goes beautifully with the fish – be sure to seek out pale, undyed haddock. If you haven't time to make your own pasta buy it freshly made, or even dried.

Serve it surrounded with a drizzle of extra virgin olive oil and a little reduced balsamic vinegar.

Serves 8 as a first course, or 4 as a main course

**12 sheets lasagne, made from the pasta
recipe** (see Basics)
1 kg smoked haddock fillets
700 ml milk
120 g butter
100 g flour
2 egg-yolks
150 ml double cream
4 tablespoons fresh coriander
seasoning

You will need a lasagne dish, circa 36 cm x 20 cm, well buttered.

Oven 150C/ 300F/ Gas 2

Cover the fish with the milk and put it into the oven for 15 minutes, then remove it and allow it to cool a little. Strain the fish, retaining the milk, and flake it, making sure there are no skin or bones left.

Make a white sauce (see Basics) with the butter, the flour and the fishy milk, adding the cream at the end and seasoning it to taste. Let it cool a little before beating in the egg-yolks. If using home-made lasagne, remove it from the cold water in which it has been resting and pat it dry with a tea towel.

Build up the dish with layers of pasta, sauce, fish and coriander. Finish with a layer of sauce and sprinkle the last few leaves of coriander on top. Bake for 30 minutes, turning the oven up to 200C/ 400F/ Gas 6 for the last 5 minutes.

Smoked Haddock Tartare

This is a most elegant first course and extremely easy to prepare. Try to find the very best, undyed haddock, which is one of our finest local fish.

Serves 4

500 g smoked haddock, skinned and carefully filleted
4 quail's eggs
rind and juice of 1/2 lemon
1 teaspoon tabasco
1 teaspoon Dijon mustard
1 dessertspoon runny honey
1 shallot, finely chopped
2 gherkins, finely chopped
1 tablespoon chives, chopped
1 dessertspoon tarragon
4 tablespoons extra virgin olive oil
seasoning
6 tablespoons of reduced balsamic vinegar
   (see Basics)
a handful of fresh herbs

For the sauce:
3 tablespoons mayonnaise (see Basics)
1 tablespoon sour cream

You will also need a round cutter, 6 cm in diameter, 5 cm in height.

With a large knife chop the fish into very small pieces – do not be tempted to use a food-processor or it will become mushy. In a large bowl, mix thoroughly the rind and lemon juice, tabasco, mustard, honey, shallot, gherkins, chives, tarragon and olive oil. Add the fish and mix it all together well. Make the sauce by mixing all the ingredients together and put everything into the fridge until you need it.

With the point of a sharp knife cut off the tops of the quail's eggs and tip the raw eggs into simmering water, stirring the water as they go in. It will set very quickly, when you can remove it with a slotted spoon and keep it in cold water until required.

To serve, put the round cutter in the middle of the plate and put a quarter of the fish mixture inside. Pat it down firmly then top it with a dessertspoon of the sauce and carefully remove the cutter. Then put a poached quail's egg on top and finally a little bunch of fresh herbs. Dribble a little of the reduced vinegar around it.

Salmon and Sea-Trout

According to the traveller Martin Martin, tradition has it that if a woman was the first to cross the Barvas River on May 1st, there would be no salmon for a full year thereafter. It would be a brave woman today who would defy such superstition. Martin also maintained that the best time for angling for salmon is 'when a warm southwest wind blows' and that the islanders 'used earth worms for bait, but cockles attract the salmon better than any other'. Today's fishermen often have different ideas.

Below, Alec (left) and Kenny Morrison. *Opposite page,* scaling a salmon.

There is a six-loch system at Amhuinnsuidhe, from which we are able to take our own sea-trout. Salmon, of course, is fished throughout the season, from the sweet river which gives the castle its name and from other fine rivers in the surrounding hills. To tell the difference between the two, look at the spots: sea-trout have more of them than salmon and slightly blunter

heads. The fish have similar life cycles, both beginning their existence in fresh water, where they stay for between two and three years before heading for the sea. The salmon swim right up to the North Atlantic, to the cold waters around Greenland, the Faroes and Norway but the sea-trout don't travel so far, possibly no further than 30 or 40 miles, feeding on the crustaceans which gives the fish its characteristic pink flesh. Another difference is that the sea-trout return every year to the rivers, while only between five and ten per cent of the salmon come back a second time.

The salmon is widely considered to be the King of Fish and the sea-trout its poor relation. Yet, possibly because it is a more 'local' fish, to a man like Mark Bilberry of the Fishery Trust the sea-trout has a right to the title – and indeed it has a truly wonderful, delicate flavour. It is very seldom farmed, whereas farmed salmon is widely available (though distinctly different from its wild cousin in taste). Finally, a salmon is a slightly larger fish: an 8-lb salmon is a commoner sight than an 8-lb sea-trout, which would be rare indeed. Though I refer to these fish in these recipes as salmon, they would be just as good with sea-trout. For me, the perfect weight is about 5 lbs (2.3 kg).

It is wonderful at Amhuinnsuidhe to see the salmon and sea-trout leaping the rock face up to the river, making their way to the lochs. One tradition at the castle (which I really appreciate) insists that the first of these fish to be caught in the season finds its way to our kitchen – whoever owned the rod that snared it.

We use this fish in so many ways – for gravadlax, for example or in any of the following recipes. However with fish this fresh, little or no cooking is required. You can sear it briefly in a hot pan, or eat it raw, as sushi.

Poached Sea-Trout
with Spring Vegetables

This is one of the simplest and best ways of preparing sea-trout or salmon. If you can't find baby fennel, use ordinary bulbs, cut small – or indeed any young, fresh spring vegetables.

Serves 4

4 sea-trout fillets, each weighing about 200g
1 litre fish stock (see Basics)
200 g butter
1 teaspoon coarse sea salt
20 small new potatoes
120 g sugar-snap peas
12 baby carrots
4 baby fennel, halved lengthwise
100 ml dry vermouth
120 ml double cream
salt and white pepper
sprigs of fennel for garnish

Oven 200C/ 400F/ Gas 6

After making quite certain that no bones have been left in the fish, put them in a large buttered dish, not touching each other. Sprinkle the sea salt over them and pour in the stock. Cover the whole thing in tinfoil and bake it for 8–10 minutes.

Boil the new potatoes and, while they cook, prepare the other vegetables: boil the carrots for a minute, or until just tender, then strain them, saving the water to do the same with the peas and finally the fennel. Mix the potatoes with all the other vegetables and 50 g butter, seasoning with salt and white pepper to taste.

When the fish is ready, measure 300 ml of the stock in which it was poached into a small pan. Reduce it to one third then add the vermouth and reduce it again. Beat in the remainder of the butter and finally stir in the cream and seasoning.

Divide the vegetables into 4 portions and arrange them, prettily, with the fish on top, surrounded by sauce and garnished with sprigs of fennel.

Salmon Fish Cakes

These little things are useful and always popular – perhaps because they remind us of childhood. But the taste is as sophisticated as you want it to be, depending on the flavouring. This recipe uses salmon but you can easily make the cakes with haddock, crab or almost any other fish.

Serves 4, generously

500 g cooked salmon
500 g mashed potato
2 egg-yolks
1 tablespoon parsley, chopped
1 tablespoon coriander, chopped
zest of 1 lemon
a pinch of chilli powder (or more, to taste)

seasoning
60 g flour
3 whole eggs, beaten
100 g white breadcrumbs
90 g butter

Mix the first 8 ingredients together thoroughly in a large bowl, using your hands. Shape them into little patties and, if you have time, leave them in the fridge for an hour to become firm.

Assemble three bowls, the first containing flour, the second the eggs and the third the breadcrumbs. Dip the patties in each bowl, in that order and fry them gently in butter for 3 minutes on each side.

Gravadlax

This means of curing salmon gets its name from the Scandinavian method of burying the fish, with spices, to preserve it. The taste is more delicate than smoked salmon and it really is remarkably easy to make, provided you begin it three days before you'll be needing it. Ask your fishmonger to prepare the fish by descaling and filleting it, removing the head, tail and fins but leaving the skin on. You should be left with two matching fillets.

Serves at least 12

1 whole salmon, filleted and prepared as above, weighing in the end 2–2¹/₂ kg
1 dessertspoon whole white peppercorns, crushed
150 g coarse sea salt
180 g granulated sugar
4 tablespoons dill, chopped
zest of 2 lemons

For the sauce:
2 egg-yolks
2 tablespoons Dijon mustard
juice of 1 lemon
1 dessertspoon caster sugar
280 ml sunflower oil
1 rounded tablespoon dill, finely chopped

Start with the marinade. Mix the pepper, salt, sugar, lemon zest and half the dill together (1). Make sure that there are no bones remaining in the fish. Put one fillet, skin-side down onto a large doubled sheet of tinfoil. Spread the mixture on top of it (2) and cover it, like a sandwich, with the other fillet, flesh-side down. Wrap it up well and put it on a large dish or tray in the fridge.

Leave it for at least 2 days and nights, turning it every 8 hours and pouring away the liquid.

Open the parcel, separate the fillets and scrape off (3) and discard the marinade-mixture (don't be tempted to wash it off). Sprinkle the remaining dill all over the surface and pat it down (4). Replace the salmon in the fridge, sandwiched in the same way and wrapped in clean foil.

To make the sauce, whisk the yolks and mustard together and add the oil drop by drop, as for mayonnaise, until it thickens. Beat in the lemon juice, sugar, dill and seasoning to taste.

Finally, slice the gravadlax thinly on the slant, starting at the tail-end (5 and 6). Serve with the sauce and toasted brioche (see Basics).

Wild Salmon
with Sorrel and Courgettes

One of the joys of living on Harris is the availability of wild salmon: it is a real treat, particularly when the fish spends practically no time between the rod and the pan! You must be very careful not to overcook it so as not to lose the delicate subtlety of its flavour.

Serves 4

4 salmon fillets, skinned, each weighing
   170–180g
60g clarified butter (see Basics)
1 teaspoon fine sea salt
Hollandaise sauce (see Basics)
4 medium courgettes
100 g sorrel leaves
4 good sprigs thyme
60 g butter
juice of 1/2 lemon

Check that there are no bones left in the fish and sprinkle each with sea salt. Wash the sorrel and remove the stalks. Cut the courgettes into thin ribbons. Over a high heat cook the vegetables in the butter for no more than a couple of minutes, then stir in the thyme leaves and lemon juice.

Fry the salmon for a minute and a half on each side, over a medium/low heat in clarified butter (I think it is nicer to have them slightly under-done, but if you disagree, cook them for a little longer).

Make a little bed of vegetables in the middle of each plate and rest the salmon on top, surrounded by the sauce.

Chicken
& Rabbit

Chicken

'Je veux qu'il n'y ait si pauvre paysan en mon royaume qu'il n'ait tous les dimanches sa poule au pot.'

Henri 1V (1553–1610)

Many an island housewife still keeps a few chickens at home to supplement the family diet. As it is probably the most widely available and versatile meat in the country, I have included several chicken recipes here, as well as one using the baby chicken, or poussin.

Scalpay Chicken

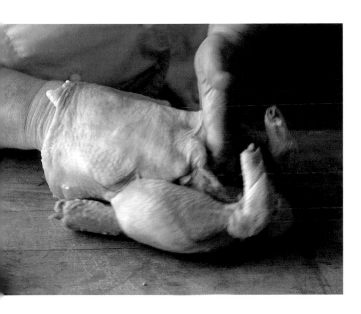

The name of this dish is a shocking pun. The little island of Scalpay lies off the coast, quite close to the castle at Amhuinnsuidhe: the chicken is virtually scalped. It is a mighty tasty variant on plain roast chicken, but you do have to get your hands messy. Should you prefer it, you can cook baby poussins the same way, though they would not take so long to cook.

Serves 6

1 large chicken, weighing about 2 kg
4 rashers smoked bacon, roughly chopped
180 g cold butter
a large bunch of tarragon
a large bunch of parsley
1 small onion
2 cloves garlic
zest of 1 lemon
seasoning

Oven 180C/ 350F/ Gas 4

Put all the ingredients except the chicken into a food-processor and mix them thoroughly. Lift the skin off the breast of the chicken, and around the top of the legs, until it is loose. Smear as much of the mixture as will fit between the skin and the meat and then the rest on top, covering it thoroughly.

Roast, uncovered, for 2 hours, basting it occasionally. Serve it with glazed parsnips and spring greens.

Glazed Parsnips

Serves 6

4 large parsnips, cut into batons, about 5 cm long
70 g butter
1 dessertspoon caster sugar

Par-boil the parsnips until just soft. Drain them and turn them in melted butter, with the sugar. Fry them for a few minutes until they are golden.

Chicken Mirin

You can steep the chicken in this marinade overnight and then barbecue it, if you like, but I often do it this way instead. The sake and mirin give it an oriental flavour and are readily available in most good supermarkets.

Serves 4

4 chicken legs, boned and flattened
olive oil
seasoning

For the marinade:
125 ml soy sauce
140 ml sake
150 ml mirin
2 cm root ginger, grated
40 g caster sugar

Mix the marinade ingredients together and allow it to infuse for half an hour before straining it. Season the chicken and fry it in olive oil until nicely browned. Pour the marinade over it and let it simmer for 5 minutes, then remove the chicken and reduce the sauce to about a third. Return the meat to the pan and simmer it for a further 5 or 10 minutes, turning it frequently until it has become glossy. Serve it with an oriental salad.

Oriental Salad

The dressing I use for this is magnificent and, what's more, will keep for up to a month in the fridge.

Serves 4

1/2 Chinese cabbage, shredded
250 g bean sprouts
1 small tin of water chestnuts, drained and finely sliced
1/2 a tin of small tin bamboo shoots, drained and cut into julienne strips
150 g mange-tout, sliced lengthwise

For the dressing:
1 tablespoon olive oil
1 tablespoon sesame seed oil
1 tablespoon soy sauce
1 tablespoon mirin
zest and juice of 2 limes
1 red chilli, deseeded and finely chopped
2 spring onions, finely chopped
1 clove garlic, finely chopped
1 dessertspoon caster sugar
seasoning

Make the dressing first, by combining all the ingredients and leaving it for an hour or two for the flavours to develop. Plunge the mange-tout into boiling water for half a minute, then refresh them. Toss them with all the other ingredients in a large bowl, with the dressing.

Chicken and Potato Pie

This is always a favourite at Amhuinnsuidhe and my 'graduates' report great success with it.
It is easier to slice the potatoes finely if you use a mandolin.

Serves 6–8

500 g puff pastry (see Basics)
4 large chicken breasts, boned and cut into thin strips
720 g peeled potatoes, thinly sliced
130 g butter
3 shallots, finely chopped
2 tablespoons tarragon leaves
2 tablespoons chives, chopped
2 egg-yolks, lightly beaten
240 ml double cream
seasoning

It helps to have a baking-mat, in which case don't bother to butter the tray but put the pastry directly onto the mat.

Oven 180C/ 350F/ Gas 4

Turn the potatoes in half the butter over a gentle heat until they are just tender – don't let them brown. Remove them from the pan and allow them to cool in a large bowl. Meanwhile, soften the shallots in the remaining butter and add the herbs and chicken, turning it over a steady heat for a few minutes until it is partially cooked. Mix it all carefully with the potatoes, season to taste and again, allow it to cool.

Roll half the pastry into a circle about 36 cm in diameter and put it straight onto a lightly buttered baking tray. Brush the edges with egg-yolk then pile the mixture in the middle. Roll the rest of the pastry into a slightly larger circle and cover the pie with it, sealing and crimping the edges. Cut a little circle in the top (about 10 cm diameter) to make a lid, leaving it in place. Brush the whole surface with the rest of the egg-yolk.

Bake the pie for about 50 minutes, checking that it's not too brown – in which case turn the oven down slightly. Heat the cream. Take the pie out of the oven, remove the lid and pour in the boiling cream, lifting the mixture gently to allow it to permeate the pie. Return it to the oven for 10 minutes.

Chicken Taransay

This takes a bit of time to prepare, but it is not expensive and it is unusual – and you can do very nearly all of it in advance (as far as the ✱). It is worth the effort, for the flavour is wonderful. The boning can be a little tricky, so it is as well to stay friendly with your butcher: the skin has to be kept intact, save for one incision underneath, as it is to be used for wrapping.

Serves 4

4 whole chicken legs, boned
8 slices Parma ham
12 chicken livers, sinews removed
1 clove garlic, finely chopped
1 dessertspoon fresh thyme
1 dessertspoon fresh sage leaves (halve this,
  if using dried herbs)
seasoning
extra virgin olive oil

You will also need string.

Oven 200C/ 400F/ Gas 6

Dry the livers thoroughly with kitchen paper and toss them in the thyme, sage and garlic. Spread the chicken legs flat, with the skin underneath and season them. Cover each with 2 slices of Parma ham and then 3 chicken livers down the centre (1). Bring the sides in slightly and gently bring the skin up to make a parcel (2). Make a sausage shape, using several pieces of string crosswise and one lengthwise (3). ✱

Brush the little bundles with olive oil and roast them uncovered, for about 40 minutes, then allow them to rest for 5 minutes before removing the string and cutting each into about 6 slices.

Serve them with buttered noodles and a crisp salad.

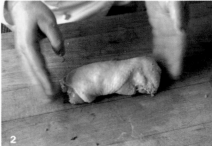

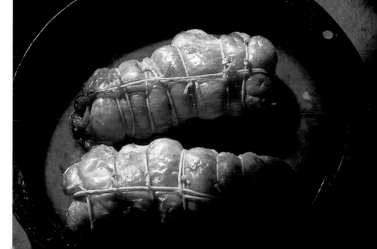

Poussins with Chestnuts

Though the quantities given here will serve four, this is a very well-behaved dish and good for a party, as it can be prepared well in advance and will sit in the oven for ages, coming to no harm. You can adapt it for chicken, pheasant or almost any poultry, but remember that it's a good idea to start it the night before you need it, to give the marinade a chance to do its valuable work.

Serves 4

4 poussins, boned and quartered (you can often buy them ready boned, or you can bone them yourself: if you do, be sure to leave the skin intact and each breast still attached to the wing)
16 very thin slices of streaky bacon
2 tablespoons olive oil
1 dessertspoon flour
2 tablespoons port
2 tablespoons redcurrant jelly
230 ml double cream

For the marinade:
1 stick celery (choose a head of celery with decent leaves, which you can use as decoration)
1 small leek
1 carrot
1 onion
2 cloves garlic
$2/3$ **bottle red wine** (sip the rest while cooking; it lubricates the voice and liberates the emotions!)

For the garnish:
12 baby onions
2 sticks of celery, chopped diagonally into lozenge-shaped pieces
1 tin cooked chestnuts (not purée)
30 g butter
1 dessertspoon caster sugar

Oven 200C/ 400F/ Gas 6

Prepare the marinade: chop all the ingredients and mix them with the wine in a large bowl. Wrap each piece of poussin with 4 slices of bacon. Secure each parcel with a cocktail stick and put them into the marinade for several hours (ideally overnight).

Strain the marinade into a jug. Take out the pieces of poussin and dry them. Heat the oil in a heavy casserole and turn the poussin pieces in it until nicely browned. Then remove them with tongs or a slotted spoon and put them aside for a minute. Put the vegetables from the marinade into the casserole, turn them over the heat, then sprinkle them with the flour and add the marinade. Bring the mixture up to boiling point, then return the poussins to the pot. Put the lid on the dish and cook it in the oven for 45 minutes (larger birds need more time).

Meanwhile prepare the garnish: cook the onions and celery in boiling, salted water for 3 minutes. Refresh them in cold water and set them aside.

When the poussins are ready, remove them from the casserole to a serving dish, being sure to remove the cocktail sticks and finish the sauce. Pour the remaining contents of the casserole through a sieve and return it to a clean saucepan over a low heat. Stir in the port, the redcurrant jelly and the cream.

If you want to serve it straight away, finish the garnish now: melt the butter with the sugar in a small frying pan, and add the onions, chestnuts and celery pieces, turning them over the heat for a few minutes, to give them a golden, caramelised character.

If you want to keep it warm, lower the oven heat and put the poussins back into the casserole until you are ready. Then pour the sauce over the poussins and arrange the garnish on each plate.

Rabbit

Country people have always known the food value of rabbit, often picking off a couple for the pot at sunset. In recent years, however, it has disappeared from more sophisticated menus. It is time for it to return.

It is available all year round, both wild and from the butcher's, though wild rabbit tends to taste gamier than its tame relations, and can be tougher: it is therefore more suitable for long, slow cooking. As in most parts of Britain, rabbits have long made their homes in the Hebrides and formed a basic element of the diet, though in recent years the proliferation of wild mink has reduced the population. The only kind of rabbit I would not recommend for the pot is a family pet – but then, it is always a nasty thought to eat anything to which you have given a name.

Many people are daunted by the problems of preparing rabbit. If it seems too much for you, your butcher might well help but if you are prepared to give it a try, it's not really very difficult if you follow these instructions.

Start by cutting the skin above the back feet and inside the rabbit's thighs. Then peel it up and pull it rapidly off the body: it should come all in one piece. Remove the head. Slit the carcass up the middle and remove the insides, discarding all of them except the liver and the kidney.

Cut off the legs and the shoulders and you are left with the saddle. If you intend to casserole the rabbit, just chop that into 4 pieces; if you need to use it whole, cut between the 4th and 5th ribs and remove the ribs, carefully sliding your knife underneath so as to keep as much meat as possible. Then remove the backbone, pulling it away so that the saddle remains intact. It is now ready for stuffing.

Rabbit with Prunes

This recipe is adapted from one I first came across in the South of France, where prunes are widely used in savoury dishes. It is a rustic, hearty dish, best eaten with plain boiled rice.

Serves 6

2 rabbits, cut into joints
2 onions, finely chopped
450 g Agen prunes, pitted
3 bay leaves
flour for dredging
olive oil
1 litre chicken stock (see Basics)
seasoning
1 dessertspoon fresh thyme

Oven 150C/ 300F/ Gas 2

Soften the onions in one tablespoon of olive oil and remove them, putting them into a large casserole dish. Dredge the rabbit in flour, shaking off the excess and sear it well on all sides before adding the softened onions. Add the bay leaves, seasoning and just enough stock to cover the contents. Cook it for an hour before adding the prunes and cooking for a further hour, or until tender.

Sprinkle the thyme over the top before serving.

Saddle of Rabbit
with Chicken Mousse and Black Pudding

On page 84, you can read of ways of dealing with these animals if you acquire them whole. In this recipe, I assume you have already skinned and prepared them – or asked your famously friendly butcher to do it for you. The joints can be used for rabbit with prunes.

Serves 4

the fillets of 2 saddles of rabbit, all skin and
   bones removed
160 g chicken breast
250 g black pudding, cubed
1 small egg-white
160 ml double cream
1/2 red pepper, deseeded, skinned and diced
   (as on page 29)
12 thin slices Parma ham
butter
seasoning

For the sauce:
1 rasher bacon, chopped
1 leek, finely chopped
1/2 bottle white wine
170 ml brandy
200 ml chicken stock (see Basics)
60 g butter
1 dessertspoon redcurrant jelly
175 ml double cream
seasoning

Oven 220C/ 425F/ Gas 7

Start by making the mousse. Process the chicken breast, add the egg-white and then carefully 'pulse' in the cream. Pass the mixture through a sieve, a spoonful at a time and chill it for half an hour. Meanwhile, sear the black pudding – very briefly and rapidly – in a little butter; drain and cool it on kitchen paper. When it is cool, fold it into the mousse mixture, with the red pepper and chill it again, for another hour or until really firm.

Spread 3 slices of Parma ham on a sheet of buttered tinfoil, 28 cm square (1), and lay the rabbit fillets, parallel, on top. Season. Spoon the mousse down the centre (2) and fold the ham up around the edges and the ends, making a long sausage of each rabbit. Roll each up in foil, like a cracker (3), and leave them in the fridge to become firm. Roast all 3 sausages in a roasting tin, to which you have added a little water, for about 30 minutes.

To make the sauce, soften the leek and bacon in 20 g butter then add the wine and 120 ml brandy. Bring it to the boil and reduce it to a third, then add the stock and reduce again to a third. Finally add the cream, the redcurrant jelly and the rest of the brandy. Simmer it for a further 5 minutes before passing it through a fine sieve and beating in the last of the butter. Serve the rabbit with buttered tagliatelle and baby leeks.

Game

Game Birds

On Harris as everywhere else in Scotland the shooting of game-birds is a seasonal event. On the 'glorious' twelfth of August the shooting of grouse and snipe opens, but in Harris I find that grouse have not yet grown large enough to be really useful until a little later.

Grouse are one of many species of game birds living living on Harris: though they cannot be hand-reared, they need protection from predators and have to be managed. The mistake people often make with grouse is to overcook it, which only makes it tough and dry. I consider that the only way to eat it is the traditional way, for which I have provided a recipe.

Snipe are not resident, but are sometimes intercepted in the course of their migration from Scandinavia to the West Country. Though they are very tiny they are delicious and considered a great delicacy. Again, they take very little time to cook.

Partridge are in season from September 1st until the end of January, along with golden plover, wild geese and wild duck: we seldom use the plover or the wild goose, but we do use a lot of mallard and partridge, always looking for the younger, more tender birds. Partridge are reared on Harris and released at the age of 8 weeks, though a few 'calling-birds' are kept back to ensure that the rest return for food. The meat of a partridge is very pale and distinctive in flavour but it tends to dry out rapidly so that it has to be carefully cooked.

Lily MacDonald's Snipe

Lily MacDonald came to Amhuinnsuidhe as a winner of a cookery competition which appeared in the pages of *The Stornoway Gazette.* She worked for many years as cook on the estate at Morsgail Lodge, in Lewis, where snipe was always a popular dish. This is a variant on her recipe. Snipe are very tiny birds and you really need two each… and finger bowls.

Serves 4 as a main course

8 snipe, plucked and trussed (see Glossary)
8 small potato cakes (see below)
12 small turnips, turned (see Basics)
8 sprigs of thyme
1 tablespoon olive oil
60 g butter

For the sauce:
1 rasher smoked bacon, diced
1 leek, finely chopped
1 clove garlic, chopped
1 shallot, chopped
1/4 bottle red wine
250 ml game stock (see Basics)
50 g butter
15 g bitter chocolate
seasoning

Oven 230C/ 450F/ Gas 8

Sear the snipe on all sides in a mixture of oil and 30 g butter and put them, seasoned, into a roasting pan, a sprig of thyme tucked into each. Boil the turned turnips and refresh them.

Make the sauce by softening the bacon, leek, garlic and shallot in 30 g butter, then adding the wine and allowing it to reduce by half. Add the stock and reduce again by half. Just before serving, stir in the chocolate and the remaining 20 g butter.

Roast the snipe for 8 minutes. Meanwhile fry the turnips in 30 g butter, with a little seasoning. Serve each snipe on a potato cake, accompanied by the turnips and the sauce.

Potato Cakes

450 g waxy potatoes, peeled
4 very thin slices bacon, finely chopped
75 g clarified butter (see Basics)
seasoning

Grate the potatoes on a coarse grater. Fry the bacon (not too crisply, as it is to be cooked again) and drain it on some kitchen paper. Mix the bacon, potatoes and clarified butter together in a bowl and sear them in a hot, non-stick pan, in little spoonfuls, patting them into cakes and turning them until they are completely cooked.

Partridge
with Celeriac and Potato Galettes

The smoky flavour of celeriac is a perfect complement to a roast partridge and the dish is elevated to grandeur by its magnificent sauce. The celeriac is an ugly brute but don't be put off.

Serves 4 as a main course

4 young partridges
4 thin rashers bacon
4 sprigs rosemary

For the celeriac and potato galettes:
1/2 large celeriac
1 large potato
60 g clarified butter (see Basics)
celery salt

For the sauce:
1 leek, chopped
1 rasher bacon, chopped
45 g butter
1/4 bottle dry white wine
300 ml game stock (see Basics)
100 ml Armagnac
50 ml fresh orange juice

Oven 230C/ 450F/ Gas 8

Check that the partridges are clean and properly plucked before trussing them with the bacon on top and the rosemary tucked inside, ready to roast.

Make the sauce by softening the leek and bacon in 30 g butter, before adding the wine. Boil briskly to reduce it by half then do the same with the game stock, this time reducing it to a third. Then add the Armagnac and the orange juice and reduce again, finally beating in the remaining 15 g butter.

Peel the celeriac and the potato and coarsely grate them. Mix them together in a bowl with the clarified butter and celery salt and allow the mixture to solidify a little. Make little flattened galettes from the mixture and fry them on a low heat, very gently as they will be quite loose, until they are golden brown.

Roast the partridges for 15–20 minutes. Let them rest for 10 minutes then remove the breasts and legs and put them back for a minute or two before serving them, on top of the celeriac and potato galettes, surrounded by the exquisite sauce.

Traditional Roast Grouse

There are no real grouse-moors on Harris, but we 'walk-up' some grouse in the summer, which produces a variable number of birds a year. If you are offered the choice, select young ones, which will be sure to be succulent. For me, there's only one way of eating grouse, which is set out below. You can prepare it all in advance, up to ✳.

Serves 4

4 young grouse, trussed (see Glossary)
4 rashers streaky bacon
4 slices white bread
120 g clarified butter (see Basics)
4 sprigs thyme
olive oil
bread sauce (see Basics)
2 tablespoons toasted breadcrumbs
seasoning

For the sauce:
1 stalk celery, finely chopped
1/2 leek, finely chopped
1 shallot, finely chopped
60 g butter
1/2 bottle red wine
400 ml game/chicken stock (see Basics)
110 ml blackberry purée
1 tablespoon rowan jelly

Oven 220C/ 425F/ Gas 7

Truss each grouse with bacon on the breast and a sprig of thyme in the cavity. Sprinkle salt and pepper on top. Cut the bread into 8 cm circles, brush them on both sides with clarified butter and bake them for 5 minutes until they become large golden brown croutons, turning them if necessary. Remove them and allow them to cool on a rack.

Next prepare the sauce: soften the leek, shallot and celery in 30 g of the butter and add the wine and then the stock, reducing by half after each addition. Stir in the purée and the jelly and reduce again until it reaches a good consistency, then season it to your taste and strain it through a fine sieve. ✳

Sear the grouse on all sides in hot oil and then roast them for 15 minutes, turning them every 5 minutes (if you prefer your grouse less pink, cook them for 5 further minutes but no more). Remove them, cut off the string and allow them to rest for a further 10 minutes. Finish the sauce by whisking the remaining butter into it. Serve each bird on a crouton, with bread sauce, toasted breadcrumbs and game chips, accompanied by the sauce.

Game Chips

A deep fryer is useful for this, but you can use an ordinary pan. Ideally, fry the chips twice – the first time, well in advance, until almost cooked; the second time very rapidly just before you're ready to eat.

6 large potatoes
sunflower oil
salt

Heat the oil to 190C. Cut the potatoes into very small chips and fry them briskly until golden brown. Drain them on folded kitchen paper.

Umbrian Duck

This is a real staple of the Amhuinnsuidhe kitchen. It is both easy and pleasing to make and tremendously impressive to serve. It is also very useful to have in the fridge as it can be produced at a moment's notice. You do, however, have to start some weeks in advance.

Serves 4 as a first course

**2 Barbary duck breasts, each weighing
   about 360 g**
40 g coarse sea salt
10 juniper berries, crushed
10 black peppercorns, crushed
10 allspice berries, crushed
1 bay leaf
rind of 1 orange

You will also need some cotton muslin and some string.

Cover the duck breasts, skin-side down, with the remaining ingredients (1). Put them in an oval gratin dish (or a plate), cover and refrigerate for 36 hours (2). Then scrape all the mixture off and discard it. Roll each breast into a sausage shape (3), wrap it in muslin (4) and secure it firmly with string at each end and then at intervals of 2 cm (5).

Hang it in a cool place to dry, by an open window for example (6), for 2 or 3 weeks. Then keep it in the fridge until you need it. Serve it sliced extremely thin, with a lentil salad and a special herb salad.

Lentil Salad

The quantities given are small, just enough for an accompaniment to the duck breasts, but this is so delicious on its own that I usually make three times as much.

120 g Umbrian lentils
3 cloves garlic, finely chopped
1 shallot, finely diced
2 tomatoes, skinned, deseeded and diced
1 dessertspoon fresh thyme
1 bay leaf
120 ml white wine
extra virgin olive oil
chicken stock (See basics)
seasoning

Soften the shallot in olive oil, then add the garlic, lentils, herbs and wine, with just enough stock to cover everything. Cook slowly for 45 minutes, topping up occasionally with stock if necessary. Strain and allow to cool. Then stir in the tomatoes and enough olive oil to make it shiny. Finally, season it according to your taste.

Special Herb Salad with Garlic and Walnut Vinaigrette

1 handful of rocket
1 handful of chervil
1 handful of coriander
1 handful of French parsley
a few tarragon leaves

For the dressing:
4 cloves garlic, crushed
6 tablespoons extra virgin olive oil
3 tablespoons walnut oil
juice of 1/2 lemon
seasoning

Mix the dressing ingredients in a bowl and leave to infuse for 4 hours, then strain the mixture into a jug. Carefully rinse the herbs, remove any stalks and toss them together with one tablespoon of dressing and serve the rest separately (or reserve it for another occasion).

Roast Wild Duck Breasts
with Chanterelles and a Blackcurrant Sauce

It is becoming increasingly easy to buy wild duck breasts in supermarkets without having to have the rest of the bird. You can use Barbary duck if you like. This is a very sophisticated way of preparing them.

Serves 4

2 wild ducks
450 g chanterelles
1 clove garlic, finely chopped
90 g butter
extra virgin olive oil
seasoning

For the sauce:
2 rashers streaky bacon, diced
1 leek, diced
1/2 bottle red wine
1 sprig thyme
1 clove garlic, roughly chopped
300 ml game/chicken stock (see Basics)
120 ml port
2 tablespoon blackcurrant purée
   (or 1 tablespoon Ribena)
90 g butter
seasoning

Oven 220C/ 425F/ Gas 7

Remove the breasts of the ducks and take the skin off (it should come away quite easily). Marinade the breasts in olive oil, garlic and seasoning for 2 hours. Use the rest of the birds to make the game stock (see Basics).

Prepare the mushrooms by chopping off the bottoms of the stalks and wiping the flat caps clean. Make the sauce by softening the bacon, garlic, leek and thyme in 60 g of the butter before adding the wine and then the stock, reducing by half after each addition. Pass it through a fine sieve and then stir in the port and blackcurrant purée (or Ribena) and let it simmer for 5 minutes.

Sear the duck breasts in a dry pan (they will still be coated with the oily marinade) and roast them, uncovered, for 5 to 7 minutes, depending on their size, before letting them rest for a further 10 minutes, on a rack.

Finally fry the mushrooms and season them. Cut each breast into 5 slices and serve the duck on top of a little heap of mushrooms, surrounded by the sauce.

Quail is a comparatively new entry on British menus but it is becoming increasingly popular. Originally a wild bird, it is now farmed all over the British Isles and quail's eggs are nearly as readily available as chickens'.

'We loathe our manna, and we long for quail.'
John Dryden (1631–1700)

Red Roast Quail
with Honeyed Spring Greens

For this recipe, the little birds are filled with a pilaff of nutty red Camargue rice which has a very distinctive taste. It can be prepared well in advance, up to the ∗ and then quickly cooked. If you are daunted by the thought of boning the quail yourself, look out for ready-boned birds in the better supermarkets.

Serves 8 as a first course, 4 as a main course

8 quail
250 g red Camargue rice
1 medium carrot
1 medium leek
1 stick celery
1 small onion
60 g butter
1 dessertspoon crème de cassis
250 ml hot chicken stock (see Basics)

You will also need a sheet of greaseproof paper, a small, very sharp knife for boning the quail, 8 thin wooden skewers and some string.

Oven 180C/ 350F/ Gas 4

Chop all the vegetables into very tiny dice. Melt the butter in a roasting tin and turn the vegetables in it, warming them through. Add the rice and continue turning everything together over a low heat for a couple of minutes. Pour in the hot stock and cover the tray with the greaseproof paper, letting it rest lightly on the surface of the pilaff. Bake for 45 minutes or a little longer until the rice is tender and still slightly nutty, topping up with stock if it is drying too quickly.

Meanwhile, bone the quail. Turn each bird upside down and make an incision along its length. Cut around the bony central part of the bird and remove it, then carefully remove the longer leg-bones, always taking care not to damage any more of the skin.

When the pilaff is ready, take it out of the oven and allow it to cool. Increase the oven heat to 200C/ 400F/ Gas 6.

Spread the flattened quail skin-down onto the board. Lift the breasts up, spoon the pilaff onto the skin, put the breasts back on the pilaff. Pull the skin up around the sides and secure it by weaving the skewer through. Turn each bird on its side and tie the legs together with string, so that it looks like a minuscule turkey. ∗

Roast them for 10 minutes, then take them out and pour a spoonful of cassis over each bird. Return them to the oven for a further 5 minutes. Serve on a bed of honeyed spring greens.

Honeyed Spring Greens

500 g spring greens
1 tablespoon of runny honey
30 g butter

Shred the spring greens finely. Blanch them for a minute and refresh them. When you're ready to serve warm them in the butter over a low heat then add the honey and seasoning. Cook gently for 2 or 3 minutes.

Aunty's Quail

One day, long before I went to work for him, I was bold enough to ring Pierre Koffmann, just to tell him how much I admired his work. We talked about food for a while and out of that conversation a recipe was born. I have named it in appreciation of his wonderful restaurant Tante Claire and in gratitude for his help.

Serves 4

6 quail
500 g puff pastry (see Basics)
4 large Savoy cabbage leaves, blanched and refreshed
1 large chicken breast, weighing 150 g
1 small egg-white
150 ml double cream
2 egg-yolks
seasoning

For the sauce:
1 rasher bacon, chopped
1 leek, chopped
30 g butter
6 medium mushrooms, quartered
250 ml white wine
300 ml quail/chicken stock (see Basics)
120 ml cream
150 ml Armagnac
a few tarragon leaves
seasoning

Oven 200C/ 400F/ Gas 6

Cut the breasts and the legs off the quail. Make 300 ml stock from the other bones (see Basics). Take the skin off the breasts and season the meat. Take the central cores out of the cabbage leaves and dry them. Set them aside while you prepare a mousse. Process the chicken breast with the egg-white, blending it really thoroughly. Carefully add the cream, using the 'pulse' button so that it doesn't curdle. Season the mixture.

Roll out the pastry thinly. Cut 4 discs, 9 cm in diameter and then another 4, 12 cm in diameter. At the centre of each smaller circle put a small piece of cabbage and 2 quail breasts. Spoon some mousse on top of this, followed by one more quail breast and a little more mousse (1). Cover it all with more cabbage and paint egg-yolk around the rim before putting the larger circle of pastry on top, pressing it gently together to make a small, round parcel and trimming the edges (2).

With a little icing-nozzle – or a very sharp knife – cut a hole from the top to allow steam to escape (3), brush egg-yolk all over the top and bake on a buttered tray for 30 minutes (4).

Make the sauce by softening the bacon and leek in butter. Add the wine and the mushrooms and reduce to a third before adding the quail stock and reducing again. Add the Armagnac, reducing a last time. Finally add the cream and seasoning. Sear the quail's legs on all sides and roast them for 15 minutes. Serve 3 around each little pie, surrounded by the sauce, garnished with a little fresh tarragon.

Venison

Red deer roam freely over the high hills of Harris. The herds are carefully tended by Kenny Morrison, his brother Alec and Roddy Macleod, grand stalkers all. The season for stags runs from August to mid-October and the season for hinds follows on over the winter, until February 15th.

The meat is sweet and tender, with very little fat; we hang it for 2 or 3 days and then use it in various ways. I like to cook the saddle, mostly – which comprises the fillet and loins – but the haunch is good for slow roasting and casseroles while meat from the shoulder or the flank makes an unusual terrine.

Although there is not much red deer available outside Scotland, other varieties, such as the fallow and the sika, are becoming more widely farmed elsewhere in the British Isles, and their meat is also delicious.

Loin of Venison
with Red Cabbage

Don't waste this scrumptious dish on anyone but your very best friends. This cut of venison comes from a saddle and is tastier than the very best fillet steak. Ask your butcher if you can have the bones for stock.

Serves 4

2 pieces of loin of venison, weighing about 600 g in all
1 medium red cabbage, very finely shredded
90 g butter
1 large onion, chopped very small
4 slices bacon, chopped very small
2 apples, peeled and diced
4 tablespoons red wine vinegar
4 tablespoons clear honey
3 level teaspoons salt
pepper
2 tablespoons olive oil
1 rounded tablespoon marmelade
225 g blueberries (optional)

For the sauce:
1 rasher smoked streaky bacon, chopped
1 leek, finely chopped
1/2 bottle red wine
300 ml venison/game stock (see Basics)
1 dessertspoon rowan jelly
120 ml port
70 g butter
seasoning

Oven 230C/ 450F/ Gas 8

Start with the cabbage. Over a low heat, melt the butter and add the onion. After a minute or two, add the bacon, followed by the cabbage, apples, honey and vinegar. Set it over a very low heat for an hour, stirring occasionally, topping up with a little chicken stock if necessary. Finally add the salt, pepper, marmelade and blueberries.

Next prepare the sauce. Soften the bacon and leek in 40 g of the butter and cook it gently for 15 minutes. Add red wine and reduce to a third then add the stock and the rowan jelly and reduce it again, this time to half, so that the sauce is developing a thicker consistency. Pass it through a fine sieve into a clean pan. Add the port and salt and pepper to taste.

Prepare the venison by removing any trace of fat or sinew, then sear it in hot olive oil. Roast for 8 minutes, until it is just firm to the touch, while you finish off the sauce by beating the remaining 30 g butter into it. Slice the meat and serve it on a bed of red cabbage, ideally with baby onions and potato purée. If you really want to impress, you could scatter a few extra blueberries around the plates.

Medallions of Venison
with Spinach and Morel Sauce

Morels are extremely expensive, but the recipe works quite well with other wild or forest mushrooms.

Serves 4

**2 pieces of loin of venison, weighing about
   600 g in all**
500 g fresh spinach
100 g butter
1 shallot, finely diced
30 g dried morels
1 rasher smoked bacon, chopped
1 leek, chopped
1/4 bottle red wine
2 tablespoons brandy
150 ml double cream
olive oil
seasoning
4 sprigs fresh thyme for garnish

Oven 220C/ 425F/ Gas7

Start by tying the loins neatly with about 8 pieces of string on each, making 2 long sausages and put them into the fridge.

Soak the morels in 200 ml of boiling water for about an hour. Then deal with the spinach: discard all the large stalks, wash the leaves well and melt them gently in 20 g butter; drain them thoroughly and set aside for later.

Start the sauce by straining the morels and reserving the water. Then soften the bacon and leek in 20 g butter, add the wine and reduce it right down to one third. Add the mushroom-water and reduce it again to about a third before stirring in the cream and brandy. Simmer the sauce for a minute, season it and strain it into a clean pan.

Sear the morels briskly for 30 seconds in 30 g butter and keep them warm while you heat the spinach, turning it gently in the rest of the butter. Sear the venison on all sides in a little olive oil and roast it for about 10 minutes. Take it from the oven and let it rest for a minute or two then remove the string and cut the meat into medallions. Serve them on top of the spinach, garnished with thyme and surrounded by the sauce and a scattering of morels.

Venison in Red Wine

This is a wonderful, warming winter dish to share with friends old or new. You need to start it the day before your party but, once made, it will wait patiently until you're ready to eat. If you can't get hold of venison, it works nearly as well with beef. I have always used a little chocolate in the sauce: it may seem odd, but it really works.

Serves 12

A haunch of venison, weighing about 7 kg
plain flour, for dredging
6 tablespoons olive oil
50 g butter
3 tablespoons redcurrant jelly
1 tablespoon port
60 g dark chocolate

For the marinade:
2 bottles red wine
2 onions, chopped
1 leek, sliced
2 carrots, chopped
2 cloves garlic, chopped
2 celery stalks, chopped
4 bay leaves
1 teaspoon peppercorns
1 small bunch parsley
4 sprigs thyme

You will also need a very large casserole dish.

Oven 200C/ 400F/ Gas 6

Ask your butcher to take the meat off the bone. Cut it into chunks, about 8 cm square, taking care to remove all sinews (save all the trimmings if you would like to use them for a venison terrine). Combine all the marinade ingredients in a large bowl and turn the meat in it. Leave it overnight.

Strain the marinade, reserving both liquid and vegetables. Remove the pieces of meat, dry them and dredge them well with flour. Heat the oil in a large frying pan and seal them in the oil over a high heat. Put them back into the heavy casserole. Melt the butter in the frying pan and add the vegetables, turning them over a gentle heat for a few minutes, then transfer them to the casserole with the meat. Pour the marinade-liquid in, put the lid on and cook it in the oven for half an hour. Then turn the heat down to 150C/ 300F/ Gas 2 and leave it to cook for a further $3^1/_2$ hours.

When the meat is very tender, strain it again, this time discarding the vegetables. Keep the meat warm while you finish making the sauce. Reduce it to half its volume over a fierce heat, then stir in the redcurrant jelly, the port and the chocolate (honestly) and reduce it further, until its consistency is creamy. Check the seasoning, pour the sauce over the meat and keep it warm in the oven until you are ready to eat. Serve with a purée of celeriac and potato and some braised chicory.

Potato and Celeriac Purée

If you've never tried cooking celeriac, do! It's one of my very favourite vegetables. This purée is rather different from ordinary mashed potato – do not be tempted to use a food-processor for the potatoes or they will become gluey.

Serves 12

1.5 kg floury potatoes
1.5 kg celeriac
180 g butter
500 ml hot milk
a pinch of nutmeg
seasoning

Peel the potatoes and boil them until soft, then sieve them and beat in half the butter followed by half the milk. Peel the celeriac, carefully removing all the fibrous matter, and cut it into rough chunks. Boil it until it is really soft then strain it and put it into a food-processor with the rest of the butter. Once it is smooth, sieve it and add it to the potatoes. Mix them well and add nutmeg and seasoning. If you feel you'd prefer it to be a little softer, add more of the milk.

Braised Chicory

Serves 12

6 heads of chicory, halved lengthwise
120 g butter
juice of 1 lemon
12 sprigs thyme
2 dessertspoons sugar
seasoning

Oven 200C/ 400F/ Gas 6

Melt the butter and lemon juice in a shallow dish in the oven. Turn the chicory in the mixture then arrange it, cut side up, with a sprig of thyme on each piece. Sprinkle the sugar over the top, cover with foil and bake for a good half-hour.

Venison Terrine

Terrines are never difficult to make and this is a very easy one. With a little salad and toast, it makes an unusual first course or light lunch, but you do need to make it the day before you serve it.

**750 g venison shoulder, trimmed of sinews and
  cut into thin strips**
750 g fatty pork, minced
3 tablespoons port
1 egg-yolk
30 juniper berries (approximately)
1 teaspoon salt
2 cloves garlic, pressed or minced
1 dessertspoon redcurrant jelly
20 very thin slices streaky bacon
a good sprinkling of pepper

You will also need some cling-film, some tinfoil and a terrine dish, ideally 26 cm x 10 cm x 7 cm.

Oven 140C/ 275F/ Gas 1

Line the terrine dish with cling-film, then with the bacon, allowing both to hang over the sides, so as to be able to wrap the whole thing up.

Put 250 g of the venison with the pork in a food-processor and process the mixture until it is smooth. Transfer it to a large bowl and add all the other ingredients, mixing it thoroughly with your hands. Transfer the mixture to the terrine dish, fold the bacon and cling-film up over the top, cover it in tinfoil and stand it on top of folded newspaper in a small baking tray.

Half-fill the baking tray with water and put it into the oven for 2 hours. Prod it with a skewer: if it emerges clean and warm the terrine is ready.

Remove the terrine dish from the water and allow it to cool for 12 hours undisturbed. Then take it from the dish, peel off and discard the old cling-film and re-wrap it in a fresh sheet. Refrigerate it until required – it can be kept in the fridge for up to a week.

Venison Carpaccio
with Black Olives and Capers

This exquisite dish works well with our venison, which is seldom hung for more than 3 days. It is absolutely essential that the meat should be trimmed clean of any trace of sinew or fat.

Serves 4 as a first course

500 g loin of venison, prepared as above
1 dessertspoon small capers
12 black olives, stoned and halved
1 small shallot, very finely diced
1 dessertspoon chives, very finely chopped
120 g fresh Parmesan cheese, in the piece
extra virgin olive oil
lots of seasoning

For the marinade:
6 tablespoons extra virgin olive oil
4 dessertspoons balsamic vinegar
salt

Cut the venison into slices about $1/2$ cm thick and put them in between two large pieces of cling-film. Bang them with a rolling-pin (but not too hard) and then roll them out, still between the sheets of film, until they become as thin as Parma ham. Put the venison in the fridge until an hour before you want to serve it.

Put the venison on plates – this is tricky, as the slices are delicate, so peel off one piece of film then invert the meat onto a plate and peel off the top layer. Sprinkle them with salt and pepper and spoon the marinade ingredients, separately, over the slices of venison.

Allow the venison to stand for about an hour at room temperature. Then sprinkle each plate with capers, olives, shallot and chives and shave fine slivers of Parmesan over the top.

Meat

Lamb

Anyone who has ever attempted to negotiate the narrow roads of Harris will know who owns the place: the black-faced sheep. Though they haven't occupied the islands for as long as have cattle, they now roam freely over very nearly every inch, with easy non-chalance. Their wool, as well as their meat, is vital to the economy.

There is a view that a little cross-breeding improves the eating quality of these sheep so that occasionally a Cheviot or a Suffolk ram is brought in for the purpose. At all events, the local custom is to prefer the meat of a wedder, or a two-year-old castrated ram. However, the demands of the mainland mean that these customs are changing a little and a certain number of lambs are now slaughtered every year from late July through to the following February. But at whatever age we eat the meat, it is particularly sweet and good because the animals feed on the wild heather that covers the moors, supplemented by the rich machair grazing on the Atlantic shore. This machair is composed of wind-blown shell sand mingled with the adjacent peat and it produces lush green grass that is used for summer grazing: some of this rich land is also cultivated, producing good crops for winter feed.

Lambs grow on the mountainside for their first summer and those not needed at home are then sold on, generally in October, to the mainland. Many small households and crofters keep a few sheep for home consumption but few would dream of killing them under the age of two. Consequently we use a good deal of mutton at the castle, which takes well to long, slow cooking.

A gigot (spelled as the French do but pronounced 'jiggut') is the cut commonly used for slow roasting while the shoulder is often salted in barrels. The custom is to preserve several pieces together, with layers of salt between them, against the long winter nights.

The mutton is cooked in water for an hour and the fat carefully skimmed off and kept, to be replaced after the salty water has been discarded and fresh water added. This is then cooked with whatever root vegetables are available: it is the basis of a Scotch broth.

Lamb with Fennel, Cardamom
and Button Mushrooms

Serves 4

1 kg lamb, from the leg, cut into 4 cm cubes
1 large onion, sliced
1 bulb fennel, sliced
300 g button mushrooms
60 g butter
zest and juice of 1 lemon
1 tablespoon whole green cardamoms
4 bay leaves
1/2 bottle white wine
150 ml crème fraîche
seasoning

Oven 170C/ 325F/ Gas 3

Sear the lamb briefly in 20 g of butter. Take it out and put the mushrooms, onion and fennel in the same pot, turning them over a gentle heat with the rest of the butter.

Return the lamb to the pot, with the vegetables and add everything else except the crème fraîche. The liquid should nearly cover the meat. If there isn't quite enough, top it up with a little stock. Cover it tightly and put it into the oven for about 1 1/2 hours, giving it a stir now and again.

Take the meat out and boil up the juices in the pan to reduce it a little then add the crème fraîche and seasoning. Serve it with rice and raisins.

Rice and Raisins

250 g Basmati rice
1/2 onion, finely diced
1 good handful raisins
1 tablespoon parsley, finely chopped
1 tablespoon fresh mint, finely chopped
120 ml white wine
chicken stock (see Basics)
olive oil
seasoning

Bring the raisins and wine to the boil together and leave them for 15 minutes to cool before draining the raisins and reserving the liquid.

Soften the onion in a little olive oil, using a large pan. Add the rice, the raisin-wine and just enough chicken stock to cover the rice by about a centimetre. Bring to the boil and simmer gently for about 15 minutes or until the rice is ready and the liquid absorbed. Stir in the raisins, parsley, mint and seasoning.

Braised Knuckle of Lamb

This dish was inspired by a visit to Effie's house where I was very taken by the delicious smell of the Morrisons' Sunday lunch: lamb, covered in sea salt and slow roasting in her Rayburn. You can prepare this well in advance, up to ∗.

Serves 6

6 large knuckles lamb
1 large carrot, roughly chopped
1 large onion, roughly chopped
8 cloves garlic (skins on)
4 sprigs thyme

1 stick celery, chopped
4 bay leaves
1 dessertspoon coarse sea salt
1 dessertspoon black peppercorns
3 dessertspoons heather honey
3/4 bottle red wine
3 level dessertspoons molasses sugar
2 tablespoons soy sauce
olive oil
black pepper

Oven 150C/ 300F/ Gas 2

Trim the knuckles so that they will stand on end, exposing the bone. Put all the vegetables and herbs into a large ovenproof dish. Sear the knuckles on all sides in olive oil and add them to the pot, standing up like soldiers in amongst the vegetables. Pour in the honey and wine and sprinkle over the salt and the peppercorns.

Cook the dish, tightly covered, in the oven for 3 hours, until the lamb is coming away from the bone.

Take the knuckles out and put them on a plate while you make the sauce. Strain and discard the vegetables and return the juices to a saucepan, stirring in the sugar and the soy sauce. Reduce the liquid until it is syrupy *.

Increase the oven temperature to 200C/ 400F/ Gas 6. Put the knuckles back into the ovenproof dish and pour some of the sauce over them, to coat them. Roast them for a further 20 minutes, basting occasionally and checking that they aren't becoming too dark – in which case cover them loosely with tinfoil.

Serve them with some butter-bean purée and small glazed onions.

Butter-bean Purée

This dish takes time to prepare but it is useful in many ways: it is lovely just eaten as it is, with crusty bread and it is very tasty as a summer salad – in which case end the recipe at **.
As with all pulses, you shouldn't add salt early in the cooking or it hardens the beans.

450 g dried butter-beans, soaked in cold water
   overnight
1 onion, roughly chopped
1 carrot, roughly chopped
2 bay leaves
6 cloves garlic

170 ml extra virgin olive oil
2 tablespoons tomato purée
2 sprigs thyme
1 level tablespoon caster sugar
seasoning

Oven 150C/ 300F/ Gas 2

Drain the beans and cover them with fresh water. Bring them to the boil and cook them for a couple of minutes before draining them again. Return the beans to the pan with the onion and the carrot and again cover them with fresh water; bring them to the boil and simmer them for about an hour – check after 40 minutes: they should be tender. Strain them, reserving the liquid.

Put the beans and other vegetables into an earthenware dish and mix in the olive oil, the garlic, bay leaves, thyme and a little of the reserved liquid, to make a thick sauce. Bake it, covered, for 40 minutes. **

Puree the mixture in a liquidiser – you may need a little more of the reserved liquid, if it seems too thick. Reheat it gently when you are ready to use it.

Rack of Lamb
with Ginger and Green Lentils

This is a lovely way to prepare young spring lamb: it is my variation on a classic dish. Trimming the lamb is important: you must be sure that the fat and the skin are removed and the bones are chopped back, to within 5 cm of the eye of the meat.

Serves 4

**4 racks of lamb, each weighing about 200 g
and trimmed**
4 dessertspoons quince jelly

For the lentils:
150 g Puy lentils
2 cm fresh root ginger, peeled and finely chopped
2 cloves garlic, finely chopped
1 shallot, finely chopped
20 g butter
1 tablespoon mint, finely chopped
100 ml white wine
400 ml lamb/chicken stock (see Basics)
seasoning

For the sauce:
1 rasher bacon, chopped
1/2 onion, chopped
1 tablespoon tomato purée
250 ml red wine
300 ml lamb stock (see Basics)
1 dessertspoon quince jelly
50 g butter

Oven 200C/ 400F/ Gas 6

Sear the lamb on the rack (where the fat is) for a few seconds until it is brown. Melt the quince jelly, slowly, in a saucepan, then cool it a little and, just as it is setting, brush it over the lamb. Sprinkle the mint over the lamb too. Chill it for an hour.

Soften the garlic, ginger and shallot in the butter, then add the lentils and the wine. Bring it to the boil and then add the stock. Simmer it gently for 15 minutes, until the lentils are tender. Strain them and season them to taste.

Roast the lamb – put it in for 15–20 minutes if you like it really rare, longer if you prefer it less pink – and allow it to rest for a further 10 minutes, while you make the sauce.

Soften the onions and bacon in half the butter then add the red wine and tomato purée and reduce it to a third. Then add the stock with the quince jelly and any juices that have run from the meat and reduce the stock again to a third. Pass it through a fine sieve before beating in the remaining butter.

Carve the racks into cutlets and serve them on a bed of lentils, with some braised chicory (see page 109) and dauphinoise potatoes.

Dauphinoise Potatoes

You can make this dish a few hours in advance
and just heat it through at the last minute. If you
like, you can cut the finished potatoes into rings,
as I do at Amhuinnsuidhe, which looks rather
smart. The quantity of cream/milk used will
depend a little on the shape of your dish: I use
one about 25 cm x 20 cm. A mandolin is useful
for slicing the potatoes, or even the fine blade
of a food-processor.

Serves 4

1 kg potatoes, peeled and very finely sliced
450 ml double cream
50 ml milk
1 clove garlic, chopped
seasoning
15 g butter

Oven 130C/ 250F/ Gas 1

Stir the seasoning and the garlic into the cream,
mixing it well and making sure it is well salted.
Butter an ovenproof dish and layer the potatoes
into it, pouring over the cream until it just covers
them. Bake it for an hour and a half, or until the
potatoes are cooked.

Saddle of Lamb
Stuffed with Kidneys and Spinach

'Have you learned to carve? For it is ridiculous not to carve well. A man who tells you gravely that he cannot carve might as well tell you that he cannot blow his nose; it is both as necessary and as easy.'
Lord Chesterfield (1694–1773)

The carving of this dish is not difficult, but the preparation takes time and care – as you might expect from such a seriously impressive party piece. Most of this preparation can be done well in advance (up to ✱). Ask your butcher to fillet and skin the lamb very carefully, keeping the skin intact and giving you the bones for use in stock (see Basics). You should be left with the loins, fillet and flank, which you will be wrapping in the skin.

In fact, there is another way of doing it, if you can get hold of about 500 g caul-fat. If you do, soak it in cold water before squeezing it out, spreading it flat like a cobweb and rolling up the lamb in it; if you do it this way, obviously you won't need the lamb's skin.

Serves 10

1 saddle of lamb, weighing about 4 kg before boning
12 slices Parma ham
2 shallots, finely chopped
800 g fresh spinach
8 lamb's kidneys
60 g butter
seasoning

For the sauce:
1 rasher smoked bacon, diced
1 medium leek, diced
60 g butter
550 ml lamb stock (see Basics)
1 tablespoon tomato purée
280 ml red wine
200 ml Madeira
1 tablespoon redcurrant jelly
seasoning
rosemary as a garnish

You will also need a lot of string, enough to tie up the meat at 2 cm intervals.

Oven 220C/ 425F/ Gas 7

Having asked your butcher to prepare the meat (see above), make sure that all fat and sinews have been removed; season it well and set it aside.

Take the long stalks off the spinach and discard them. Wash the spinach leaves thoroughly and drain them. Soften the shallots in 30 g butter and add the spinach, turning it gently over the heat until it wilts. Drain it thoroughly, pressing all the liquid from it.

Prepare the kidneys by halving them horizontally and removing and discarding the hard sinews. Sear them on all sides in the remaining butter and leave them to cool, allowing all the juices to drain away.

Spread out the skin (or caul-fat), ready for wrapping. Arrange the 2 pieces of loin on it, close to and parallel with the longer side of the skin, with a little trough between them for the stuffing. Put the fillets on top of the smaller ends of the loins, to balance them up.

Line this trough with 8 slices of Parma ham, each crossing the centre and hanging over the side (1) ready to be rolled around the spinach. Line this, again, with half the spinach. Put a row of kidneys along the trough (2) and season them well before covering them with the rest of the spinach.

Now bring up the ends of the ham to make a long sausage. Cover this with the meat from the flank and roll the whole thing up, securing it very tightly with string and using the remaining prosciutto to cover the ends (3). ✳

If you can, leave it for a few hours in the fridge to allow it to settle. Roast it for 35 minutes if you like it rare, longer if not, and allow it to stand, covered in tinfoil, on a rack, for 20 minutes, before carving.

Make the sauce by gently softening the bacon and leek in 30 g butter for 5 minutes. Then add the red wine and Madeira and reduce it to a third of its original volume.

Add the lamb stock, tomato purée and redcurrant jelly and reduce it again to a third until it becomes slightly thicker. Whisk in the remaining 30 g butter at the last minute. Serve with minty new potatoes.

Beef

'Then get me a tender sirloin
From off the bench or hook,
And lend to its sterling goodness
The science of The Cook.

And the night shall be filled with comfort,
And the cares with which it begun
Shall fold up their blankets like Indians
And silently cut and run.'

Phoebe Cary (1824–1871)

Cattle lived in the islands long before the arrival of sheep. The beef industry has, however, changed a good deal since Martin Martin wrote: 'These Cows are very little but very fruitful, and their Beef very sweet and tender'.

At one time, every croft would have had a couple of house cows and they would almost certainly have been shaggy Highlanders: when one was slaughtered, its meat was salted down to see the family through the winter.

Although these lovely creatures do still wander about the roads of Harris, the advent of domestic freezers has caused the gradual disappearance of home salting, until nowadays it is only those who hanker for a nostalgic taste of childhood who even buy salt-beef, let alone produce it at home.

Highland cattle were often crossed with Shorthorn bulls until about 20 years ago. Now, in a constant drive to improve the stock, many more continental strains have been introduced, particularly the Limousin and the Charolais, via the artificial insemination scheme organised on the mainland.

Again, slaughtering habits have changed recently: the custom was always to keep calves until they were nearly 3 years old, but today many of them don't live past 18 months.

If it seems, sentimentally, rather sad to be losing the pure-bred local beef of the islands, there is a very positive side to it. The system of improvement by cross-breeding is working. The beef we buy on Harris today may be descended from an Aberdeen Angus, by way of a Highland, a Shorthorn and a Charolais, but it is still some of the tastiest meat in the world.

Island Meatballs

This is hearty sustaining winter food.

Serves 6

1 kg rump steak, minced twice
1 large onion, finely diced
2 egg-yolks
black pepper
salt
1 teaspoon caster sugar
1 teaspoon ground ginger
1 teaspoon ground cloves
1 teaspoon allspice
olive oil

Soften the onion in a little oil then mix all the ingredients in a large bowl. Roll it into small balls, the size of golf balls, and fry them in oil until brown all over. Serve with a green salad, tomato sauce no. 1 (see Basics) and Rumbledethumps.

Rumbledethumps

If a mixture of potato and cabbage can be known as bubble-and-squeak in England it shouldn't surprise us that the Scottish version makes a heartier noise.

Here is a recipe quoted by Christopher North in his *Noctes Ambrosianae*:
'Take a peck of purtatoes and put them in a boyne – at them with a beetle – a dab of butter – the beetle again – another dab – then cabbage – purtato – beetle and dab – saut meanwhile – and a shake o' common black pepper – feenally, cabbage and purtato throughither – pree, and you'll fin' them decent rumbledethumps'.

Mine is similar.

1 kg potatoes
1 small cabbage
25 g butter
4 tablespoons grated Isle of Mull cheese, or
   any cheddar
1 tablespoon chives, chopped
1 teaspoon ground nutmeg
seasoning

Oven 220C/ 425F/ Gas 7

Boil the potatoes until soft then mash them and allow them to cool. Shred the cabbage and boil it for 3 minutes. Strain and refresh it. Mix the vegetables, chives and seasoning together with 2 tablespoons of cheese.

Melt the butter then shape the mixture into little patties – about 6 cm in diameter – and brush them all over with melted butter. Sprinkle the remaining cheese on top and bake for 20 minutes.

Beef MacLeod

We have named this splendid beef dish after the old Lords of the Isles instead of the hero of Waterloo. Highlander and Aberdeen Angus beef are especially delicious when they have been properly hung: if you can, get a cut called a strip loin instead of sirloin: although it is expensive, it is the best and there is no waste. However, the pudding is good enough to eat on its own, so if a vegetarian should stray into your Sunday lunch party, just increase the quantities.

Serves 8

sirloin of beef, weighing 1.5 kg when trimmed
1 onion, roughly chopped
1 leek, roughly chopped
a good pinch of sea salt
1 tablespoon plain flour
1/2 bottle red wine
250 ml brown stock (see Basics)
olive oil

For the pudding:
230 ml milk
180 ml cold water
2 eggs
200 g plain flour
1 Spanish onion, chopped
1 tablespoon fresh thyme
olive oil
seasoning

You will need 2 muffin trays, bun trays, or similar, for cooking the puddings.

Oven 230C/ 450F/ Gas 8

Start with the pudding. Sear the onion in olive oil until it is brown, sticky and sweet. Add the thyme and season the mixture generously. Leave it to cool. Beat the rest of the ingredients together and chill this batter for an hour, while you start on the meat.

Seal the beef in hot oil until it is browned on all sides. Scatter the onion and leek over the base of your roasting tin and put the beef on top, sprinkling the salt all over it. Roast it for 40 minutes if you like it rare, longer if you prefer it well done. It must stand for 20 minutes, covered in tinfoil, on a grid over a plate to collect the juices, before you carve it.

While it roasts, finish the pudding. Put enough oil into the trays to cover the bottom – probably about a dessertspoonful for each indentation – and heat them in the oven until smoking hot. Take the batter from the fridge and stir in the onion mixture. Remove the trays from the oven and pour the mixture in, enjoying the essential sizzle. Return the trays to the oven for about 15 minutes – check after 12.

Finally, make the gravy: sprinkle the flour over the onion and leek mixture in the base of the roasting tin and stir over the heat before adding the wine. Bring it to the boil and let it simmer for a minute before adding your stock. Simmer it again and finally pour in the juices from the beef, before straining it into a jug. This dish goes very well with rosemary potatoes.

Rosemary Potatoes

Serves 8

The success of this dish depends on your remembering to turn the potatoes several times during cooking, so that they arc crisp all over.

1.5 kg small, waxy potatoes
1 rounded tablespoon rosemary leaves
olive oil
coarse sea salt

Oven 230C/ 450F/ Gas 8

Pound the rosemary leaves in a mortar, to release their flavour. Wash the potatoes and cut thcm into wedges, like large, blunt chips. Combine all the ingredients in a roasting tray using enough olive oil to coat the potatoes and roast them for an hour, turning frequently.

Braised Oxtail

This is one of the classics of British cooking. It is the most wonderfully warming and encouraging dish to serve on a winter's night, with lashing of good red wine and fine company.

Serves 6 to 8

2.5 kg oxtail, trimmed of fat
6 rashers streaky bacon, chopped
100 ml brandy
100 g butter
olive oil
500 ml brown stock (see Basics)
fresh thyme
black peppercorns
4 bay leaves
3 tablespoons parsley
1 tablespoon plain flour
24 shallots, peeled and left whole
8 medium carrots
100 g butter
1 rounded tablespoon caster sugar

For the marinade:
2 bottles of red wine
3 medium onions, roughly chopped
3 large carrots, roughly chopped
2 sticks celery, roughly chopped
8 cloves garlic, chopped

For the garnish:
3 tablespoons lardons – or chopped bacon
2 tablespoons parsley, chopped

Oven 150C/ 300/ Gas 2

Ask your butcher to trim the excess fat off the oxtail and to discard it. Chop the oxtail into pieces and immerse them in the marinade overnight.

Remove the pieces of meat and pat them dry with kitchen paper; strain and reserve the marinade, patting the vegetables dry too, and setting them aside. Seal the meat in a frying pan, in a mixture of oil and some of the butter, browning the pieces on all sides over great heat. Put the meat aside into a very large casserole.

Wipe out the frying pan, melt some more butter and turn the dried vegetables in it until they, too, go brown. Add a tablespoon of flour to the mixture and stir it in. Add the contents of the frying pan to the meat in the casserole.

Deglaze the frying pan with the brandy and add that, too, to the pot. Next, wipe the frying pan again and fry the chopped bacon; add it to the casserole too.

Now boil up the marinade liquid in a clean saucepan and reduce by a third. Add that to the pot, with the thyme, peppercorns and bay leaves and just enough brown stock to cover the contents. Cook it in the oven for 4 hours, or until the meat comes easily away from the bone.

When it is tender, carefully remove the pieces of oxtail from the casserole and pass the sauce through a fine sieve. Stir in the sugar. Allow the fat to rise to the top and skim it off. Return the oxtail to the casserole, with the sauce.

Finally, prepare the remaining vegetables. Slice the carrots into 1 cm rounds and turn them in butter over gentle heat, with the onions, before roasting them for 25 minutes. Stir them all carefully into the casserole and reheat the whole gently.

Garnish the dish with crisply fried bacon pieces and parsley and serve with a parsnip purée.

Parsnip Purée

Serves 8

1.3 kg parsnips
60 g butter
150 ml double cream
nutmeg
seasoning

Peel, roughly chop and boil the parsnips until they are very soft. Strain them and put them into a fodd processor, add the butter and cream, but be careful not to overwork the cream. Heat the purée gently in a saucepan.

Puddings
& Baking

Crème Brûlée

'Health that is purchased by a rigorous watching of the diet is but a tedious disease.'
Baron de Montesquieu (1689–1755)

This is probably the world's most delicious pudding, superb just as it is and also very adaptable. You can put fresh raspberries or strawberries in the bases of the ramekins, or prunes soaked in Armagnac, or virtually anything else you like.

Serves 6

600 ml double cream
200 ml whipping cream
75 g caster sugar
7 egg-yolks
1 vanilla pod
extra caster sugar for the caramel

You will also need 6 ramekin dishes.

Oven 130C/ 250F/ Gas 1

Whisk the egg-yolks with the sugar until the mixture is light. Slit the vanilla pod and add the seeds to the creams, with the pod. Bring it to the boil then strain it and add it to the egg-yolks and sugar, whisking all the time. Then pour it into a jug and fill the ramekins to the top. Bake them in a bain-marie for 2 hours, or until they are set.

Remove the ramekins and allow them to cool. Then sprinkle a thin layer of sugar over the surfaces. Melt the sugar either with a blow-torch or under a fierce grill, just enough for it to caramelise. On no account keep the ramekins in the fridge or the tops will go soggy.

Chocolate Cake

'Love and gluttony justify everything'
Oscar Wilde (1854–1900)

Every cookery book needs at least one good chocolate cake: this is mine. It is deliciously moist and very adaptable: you could layer it with fruit, or dust it with cocoa or icing sugar.

Serves 8

200 g good plain chocolate
2 tablespoons freshly made coffee
1 tablespoon rum
120 g unsalted butter
130 g caster sugar
6 egg-yolks
70 g plain flour
60 g ground almonds
7 egg-whites

You will need a 23 cm cake tin, preferably loose-bottomed.

Oven 180C/ 350F/ Gas 4

Prepare the tin by buttering it thoroughly and dusting it with flour. Melt the chocolate in a bain-marie and stir in the butter, coffee and rum. Allow it to cool a little while you beat the sugar and yolks together, until pale, then beat in the chocolate mixture. Fold in the flour and ground almonds. Beat the egg-whites to soft peak and then fold them, too, into the mixture before transferring it to the tin.

Smooth the surface and bake the cake for about 45 minutes – test it with a skewer: if it comes out of the cake clean, it is ready. Let it settle in the tin for a few minutes then turn it out to cool on a rack.

Raspberries

I have used a lot of raspberries in this book, because they are so plentiful on Harris and their season goes from May right through until September.

They are grown in tunnels and their quality is unparalleled. This may be partly because climatic conditions demand that they take a long time to mature and develop their flavour. No chemical sprays are used in their cultivation and they are liberally watered by soft and wonderfully pure rain.

Strawberries are grown in similar conditions, again for a remarkably long season and they too are sweet and good. In many of the following recipes, the two are interchangeable.

Sydney Smith would have been astonished. It was he who wrote that 'no people has so large a stock of benevolence of heart as the Scotch – They would have you even believe they can ripen fruit'. . .

Raspberry soufflés.

Raspberry Soufflés

Serves 6

200 g raspberries
3 tablespoons crème pâtissière (see Basics)
8 egg-whites
45 g caster sugar
1 egg-yolk
a few drops of good vanilla essence
caster sugar for dredging

You will also need 6 ramekin dishes.

Oven 180C/ 350F/ Gas 4

Butter the ramekins very thoroughly, dredge them with sugar and put them in the fridge. Crush a third of the raspberries with a fork. Mix the crème pâtissière with the vanilla essence, the egg-yolk and the crushed raspberries. Beat the egg-whites until they form soft peaks and then add the sugar and beat again, for a few seconds. Fold one third of this into the raspberry mixture, to slacken it, and then fold in the rest, gently so as not to lose the air. Fold in the rest of the whole raspberries.

Fill the chilled ramekins to the brim. Smooth the tops and run your thumb around each, just inside the rim (this helps rising). Pop the soufflés straight into the oven for 7–8 minutes and serve them immediately, sprinkled with icing sugar.

Raspberry Tart

This simple tart is adaptable for any other fresh fruit.

Serves 6

1 quantity of rich shortcrust pastry (see Basics)
1/2 quantity crème pâtissière (see Basics)
125 ml double cream
450 g fresh raspberries
icing sugar for dusting
fresh mint leaves

Oven 200C/ 400F/ Gas 6

Roll the pastry out into a thin circle. Use it to line a buttered, loose-bottomed 23 cm flan tin. Prick it all over with a fork and bake it 'blind' for 15 minutes – the best way of doing this is to put some tinfoil on top of the pastry and fill it with either ceramic baking-beans, dried peas or rice.

Remove the foil and beans/rice and replace the tart in the oven for a further 5 minutes until it is pale gold in colour (keep an eye on it, that it does not burn).

Remove the pastry again and allow it to cool. Take it out of the tin, with great care, and put it onto a serving dish. Whip the cream lightly and fold half of it into the crème pâtissière, to loosen it. Fold in the rest of the whipped cream and spread it over the base of the tart. Fill it with raspberries. Just before serving dust it with icing sugar and decorate it with mint. Serve it with a raspberry coulis (see next page).

Lady Sophie's Meringue

The benign and gentle spirit of Lady Sophie Scott, who lived at Amhuinnsuidhe long ago, is sometimes thought to drift around the castle. I have named this wonderful pudding after her as it is beautiful, pale, and light as air. It is also remarkably easy to make. Do not be tempted by 'fat-free' crème fraîche, as it hasn't the substance for the job.

Serves 4

6 egg-whites
320 g caster sugar
1 rounded tablespoon cornflour
2 teaspoons lemon juice
240 ml crème fraîche
225 g fresh raspberries

Oven 130C/ 250F/ Gas 1

Line a shallow roasting tin (about 30 cm x 20 cm) with greaseproof paper. Whisk the egg-whites to soft peaks in a clean bowl then add half the sugar and continue whisking. Add the cornflour and the lemon juice, still whisking. Finally whisk in the remaining sugar.

Spread the mixture evenly over the tin and bake it for about 20 minutes, until the surface is beginning to crack. Remove it from the oven and allow it to cool on the tray.

Spread a clean tea towel on the table and invert the meringue onto it, then remove the tin and peel off the paper. Spread the crème fraîche on top and scatter the raspberries over it before rolling it, lengthwise, into a log, using the tea towel to help you handle it. Do not worry that the top appears cracked: it is meant to. Let it settle before putting it onto a serving dish.

An alternative way of serving this, which we prefer at the castle, is to cut circles of the meringue before (and instead of) rolling it, using a round cutter: I also beat some double cream into the crème fraîche if doing it this way and top each circle with prettily arranged raspberries and a mint leaf.

Raspberry Coulis

This can be kept in the fridge for up to 4 days and can be used to accompany sorbets, mousses, ice creams etc. The sweetness of the coulis depends on taste, so you can use more or less syrup, as you like.

Serves 6

250 g fresh raspberries
juice of 1 lemon
about 80 ml of syrup no. 1 (see Basics)

Puree the fruit and the lemon juice in a blender, pass it through a fine sieve it and then add the cold syrup.

Mousse Nouvelle

There are two special things about this glamorous pudding: one is the fact that, though very light in texture, it keeps its shape and can be sliced, almost like a cake: the other is its unusual biscuit base. It is important to use leaf gelatine, which is easier to manage and cleaner in taste than the powdered sort: soak the leaves for at least 15 minutes, in a flat baking tray or loaf-tin, until they are soft enough to squeeze.

I am very grateful to Jean-Christophe Novelli for the original idea, which I have adapted in this recipe. It works equally well with strawberry purée instead of raspberry.

Serves 8

300 g raspberries (fresh, if possible)
75 g unsalted butter
3 gelatine leaves
130 g lightly whipped cream
1 quantity biscuit base (see Basics)

For the Italian meringue:
3 egg-whites
130 g caster sugar

At the castle I use small square moulds, but you can use a 25 cm stainless-steel ring. Failing that, line a loose-bottomed cake tin with cling film (so as to avoid the metal reacting badly with the raspberries). You will also need a sugar thermometer and an electric whisk.

Cut the biscuit base so as to fit snugly inside the ring (or the tin). Soak the gelatine leaves in a bowl of cold water (see above). Rub all but a dozen of the raspberries through a fine sieve into a large bowl and put two tablespoonsful of the pulp into a small pan to warm. Squeeze the water gently from the gelatine leaves and add them to the pan, warming and stirring the mixture until the gelatine has dissolved. Stir in the butter until it too has melted and pour it into the rest of the sieved raspberries. Set it aside, stirring occasionally so that it doesn't start to set.

Make the Italian meringue: put 2 tablespoons of cold water into a small, heavy saucepan and add the sugar. Heat it gently and steadily – have a bowl of cold water and a pastry-brush handy in case crystals begin to form, in which case brush around the inside of the pan to disperse them. When it has reached 120C, set it aside and start whisking the egg-whites. When they have just reached soft peaks, add the syrup slowly and whisk continuously for 5 minutes until it is very smooth. Whisk a third of the meringue mixture into the raspberry mixture then fold in the rest, followed by the cream.

Spoon the mixture into the ring (squares, or tin) and refridgerate the mousse for at least 4 hours. Remove it from the fridge half an hour before serving, surrounded by the remaining raspberries. You could serve this with a raspberry sorbet (see next page) or a raspberry coulis (see previous page).

Raspberry Sorbet
with Tuiles

This is another very useful dish to have sitting in your freezer in the event of unexpected guests. It should be removed from the freezer about half an hour before you want to serve it. You really need an ice cream machine, but if you haven't got one, remove the sorbet from the freezer every now and again as it freezes and give it a stir to break down the crystals.

Serves 6

500 g fresh raspberries
juice of 1 lemon
1/2 quantity syrup no. 1 (see Basics)

Pass the raspberries through a fine sieve then stir in the lemon juice and add the syrup. This is a matter of taste: if you think it is sweet enough before you have finished adding it all, just stop. Either put it into an ice cream machine or freeze it, as suggested above. You could serve it with tuiles.

Tuiles

These very fine biscuits are lovely with ice cream and mousse as well as with this sorbet. They are also pretty good just on their own – but they don't keep. Eat them the day you make them. You will need a baking-mat and a sheet of plastic – say the top of an ice cream carton – out of which you have to cut a circle, about 7 cm in diameter.

75 g unsalted butter, room temperature
100 g caster sugar
35 g icing sugar, sieved
4 egg-whites
100 g plain flour

Oven 180C/ 350F/ Gas 4

Beat the butter in a mixer until it is very light. Add the caster sugar and the sieved icing sugar and beat again. Little by little, beat in the egg-whites, followed by the flour. Put the mixture in the fridge – ideally, for 4 hours.

Put your sheet of plastic (out of which you have cut a circle) on top of a baking-mat, on a tray. Spread the mixture thinly over the circle, using a palette knife. As you finish each biscuit, move the template.

When the tray is full, bake the biscuits for about 10 minutes or until golden brown. They harden rapidly as they cool, so if you want to roll them around a rolling-pin, or make baskets of them, do it as quickly as possible.

Baking

There is a long tradition of home-baking in the islands. It's economical and substantial fare but the skills involved in its production are considerable.

At the castle we are very lucky to be able to learn from Effie Morrison how to turn out some of the finest of such delicacies. In the following section, I am indebted to her for her scones, oatcakes, scotch pancakes and, of course, for her inimitable clootie dumpling.

Oatmeal has always been versatile in this part of the world. In the 17th century it was observed 'When the Cough affects them, they drink Brochan plentifully, which is Oatmeal and Water boil'd together to which they some times add butter'. We tend to use whisky these days, for such purposes.

Another use for oatmeal – which is currently out of fashion – was to use it to make up a cold porridge, which you then put into your sporran and carried into battle. It has also been used for making soap, and there was once a widespread belief that 'there is a notable seasoning of phosphorus in oats which produces the praefervidum in genuine Scotsman'.

It makes very fine oatcakes too.

For oatcakes, scones or Clootie dumpling I happily hand over the apron to Effie.

Oatcakes

In the Hebrides, oatcakes are often served with croudie – a soft cream cheese. They break easily, but this crispness is part of their charm.

350 g fine oatmeal
75 g butter
1 pinch baking powder
1 pinch salt

Oven 230C/ 450F/ Gas 8

Mix all the dry ingredients in a bowl. Melt the butter in about 115 ml of water. Add this to the bowl and mix it carefully together with your hands.

Roll out the mixture very gently on a surface which has been lightly sprinkled with oatmeal and cut it into 5 cm squares. Put the squares onto a hot baking tray and bake them for 20 minutes. Turn them over and replace them in the oven for a further 2 or 3 minutes. Leave them to cool.

Shortbread

This is a very useful stand-by for unexpected visitors – or a ceilidh. In the Hebrides, a ceilidh can mean anything from a full-scale dancing-party lasting until dawn to a casual visit.
When scoring the surface, take the knife halfway through the mixture, to make breaking it easier.

200 g unsalted butter
100 g caster sugar
200 g plain flour
100 g rice flour, or fine semolina

Oven 150C/ 300F/ Gas 2

Beat the butter until its pale and creamy then beat in the sugar. Sieve the two flours and beat them in gradually. With floured fingers, press it into a tin – it should be about 1 cm deep. If you decide to use a round tin, score the surface deeply into wedges, if you use a rectangular one, score it into fingers. In either case, prick the top all over with a fork and bake it for about 50 minutes, until it is pale, golden colour.

Allow it to cool a little in the tin, then turn it out onto a wire rack.

Scones

Serves 6

360 g self-raising flour
60 g caster sugar
45 g butter
1 heaped teaspoon cream of tartar
1 level teaspoon baking powder
1 egg
150 ml milk

Oven 200C/ 400F/ Gas 6

Mix the flour and sugar in a large bowl and rub in the butter until the mixture resembles breadcrumbs. Stir in the cream of tartar and baking powder and make a well in the mixture. Pour in the beaten egg and enough milk to produce a very soft consistency and mix it all gently together, drawing in the flour mixture as you go.

Turn the mixture onto a floured surface and roll it lightly until it is about 2 cm thick. Then cut it into triangles, put them onto a buttered tray and bake them for 10 minutes. Remove them and cool them on a rack.

Scotch Pancakes

You can whip up these little pancakes in no time, especially when hungry children are around but beware, you'll never make enough.

Serves 8

250 g self-raising flour
160 g caster sugar
1 heaped teaspoon baking powder
2 eggs
30 g unsalted butter
1 tablespoon golden syrup
200 ml milk

Mix the first three ingredients and stir in the eggs. Beat the milk in gradually, to make a thick batter. Melt the butter and syrup together and add them to the batter. Heat a griddle, or large frying pan, and oil it lightly. Drop spoonfuls of the batter onto it, flipping them over as soon as bubbles appear. Serve them hot, immediately, with butter and jam if you like.

Saint Clement's Cake

I couldn't resist including this light, fresh tasting cake which is made with olive oil instead of butter. I first came across it in Tuscany, when it was made by Conte Contini Bonacossi at La Tenata di Cappezzana: it has no connection at all with the Hebrides!

3 large eggs
300 g caster sugar
300 g plain flour
165 ml milk
165 ml extra virgin olive oil
1 teaspoon grated lemon zest
1 teaspoon grated orange zest
juice of one lemon
1 tablespoon baking powder

Oven 180C/ 350F/ Gas 4

Butter and flour a 25 cm cake tin. Beat the sugar and the eggs until they are pale and creamy. Stir in the remaining ingredients and bake the cake for 30–40 minutes, until it is golden brown. Allow it to cool a little in the tin and then turn it out onto a rack. Serve it with a glass of Drambuie.

Clootie Dumpling

There's a little book of Scottish folklore by Allan Morrison called *Ye Cannae Shove Yer Granny Aff a Bus.* This interesting work of reference contains a vital section on key rules for grannies, including the resounding command 'Make Plenty of Clootie Dumpling'.

This is a substantial and splendid dish. It would make a welcome alternative to Christmas pudding. The quantities are given in cereal-bowlfuls: I could try to translate these into grams, ounces or cups, but hell, it works like this and surely everyone has cereal bowls?

Serves 12 – or more

3 bowls self-raising flour
1 packet Atora suet
1 heaped teaspoon cream of tartar
1 level teaspoon baking powder
1 bowl granulated sugar
1 teaspoon cinnamon
1 teaspoon mixed spice
1 teaspoon ginger
1 bowl sultanas
1 heaped bowl raisins
2 tablespoons golden syrup
2 tablespoons treacle
640 ml hot water (approximately)

1 large piece of cloth, about 80 cm square – cotton sheeting will do.

Set a very large pan of water to simmer on the stove, with a saucer in the bottom to take the pudding. Mix all the dry ingredients together. Add the syrup, treacle and hot water and mix it all together well. Sprinkle the cloth with water and then lightly dust it with flour. Put the pudding mixture in the middle and bring the sides up, tying it together tightly with string.

Put the pudding in the pan of simmering water: it should come three quarters of the way up the sides. Allow it to simmer gently for 3 hours, topping it up with boiling water as necessary.

Towards the end, set the oven 200C/400F/Gas 6

Take the pudding out and settle it to drain over a large colander or similar. Untie the string and slowly peel away the cloth, leaving a lovely round pudding. Before you take the cloth away completely, you'll have to invert it onto a large plate and pop the whole thing into the oven for 3 minutes to give it a crust.

Glossary

Bain-marie

The dish containing the mixture to be cooked is placed in a second larger vessel of barely simmering water. This is a method of gently baking custards, mousselines etc. where direct heat would be too strong.

To blanch

A way of cooking vegetables very briefly, before using them in recipes. Generally, the vegetables are peeled/sliced, then plunged into boiling water for a minute, before being strained and refreshed.

To deglaze

A method of cleaning a pan with another liquid, whilst retaining all the flavours it previously contained. The liquid – often wine or brandy – is poured in, brought to the boil and stirred until everything is incorporated.

Julienne

Vegetables sliced or shredded into slender matchstick shapes.

Marinade

A mixture, usually containing oil, wine, herbs, spices and other flavourings in which meat or fish are immersed before cooking.

To refresh

A way of ensuring that blanched vegetables maintain their colour and/or shape. They are strained, then immersed immediately in very cold water before being strained again and reserved for further use.

To sear

To cook rapidly over a very high heat, in order to seal in the flavour.

To skin tomatoes

Many recipes demand that tomatoes should be prepared in this way. It is quite simple: with a sharp knife, remove the core of each tomato and cut a shallow cross on the round top. Plunge them into boiling water for 20 seconds then into a bowl of cold water: the skins should slip off quite easily. To deseed them, quarter them and scoop out the pips.

To truss

To tie up a bird for roasting. Start by crossing the legs up towards the breast. Then tie the feet together with a long piece of string, which is then passed and crossed underneath the bird and tied in a bow on top of the breast.

To turn vegetables

This is a way of preparing carrots, potatoes courgettes, etc. so that they are of uniform size and shape, for a special garnish. Peel the raw vegetables and cut them into batons, about 5 cm in length. With a sharp knife pare away the corners, producing a barrel shape (see page 23).

Basics

Eggs

When eggs, egg-whites and egg-yolks are used in this book, they are all eggs of 'medium' size (unless I say otherwise).

Ovens

Do remember that all ovens are different so that cooking times may vary. Use your judgement; if it seems to you that something needs a little less or more time than the recipe suggests, you are probably right to follow your instincts. Also, ovens should always be preheated.

Butter

I like unsalted butter, so when butter is mentioned it is always the unsalted kind. Salted butter may very well work with most savoury recipes so it Is up to you. Under no circumstances should you use it for pastry!

Olive oil

I use extra virgin olive oil nearly all the time because I, personally, like it enormously. It is usually better to use the extra virgin olive oil for salad dressings but there is no need to use the very best for other purposes such as searing, sealing, frying etc...

Reducing and sieving

I sieve and reduce a lot, and you will, no doubt, be tempted to skip that part: don't, be patient, because it's important. Sieved ingredients have a finer, smoother texture. When reduced they have a much sharper, finer taste, and all this makes for fine cooking, which is what I am striving for.

Quantities

The quantities given in this book are measured in kilograms and litres. If you feel uncomfortable with metric measurements, use the following tables to convert the recipes. Such conversions are always approximate (rounded up or down) so never mix imperial and metric in the same recipe.

Solid measurements

metric	imperial	metric	imperial
25 g	1 oz	350 g	12 oz
50 g	2 oz	370 g	13 oz
85 g	3 oz	400 g	14 oz
100 g	4 oz	425 g	15 oz
140 g	5 oz	450 g	16 oz (1 lb)
170 g	6 oz	675 g	1½ lb
200 g	7 oz	900 g	2 lb
225 g	8 oz (½ lb)	1 kg	2.2 lb
255 g	9 oz	2.3 kg	5 lb
285 g	10 oz	3.2 kg	7 lb
310 g	11 oz	4.5 kg	10 lb

Spoon measurements

1 teaspoon – 5 ml spoon

1 dessertspoon = 10 ml spoon

1 tablespoon = 15 ml spoon

Liquid measurements

ml	fl oz	imperial
15 ml	½ fl oz	
30 ml	1 fl oz	
60 ml	2 fl oz	
150 ml	5 fl oz	¼ pint
190 ml	6.6 fl oz	⅓ pint
300 ml	10 fl oz	½ pint
450 ml	15 fl oz	¾ pint
600 ml	20 fl oz	1 pint
900 ml	30 fl oz	1½ pint
1000 ml (1 litre)	34 fl oz	1¾ pint

Biscuit Base

This quantity is plenty for one mousse.

100 g ground almonds
100 g caster sugar
1 egg
1 egg-yolk
25 g unsalted butter, melted
20 g plain flour
1 dessertspoon Kirsch or similar liqueur (optional)
3 egg-whites
1 dessertspoon caster sugar

You will also need baking parchment, or a 'magic carpet' baking sheet.

Oven 200C/ 400F/ Gas 6

In a large bowl, combine the first 6 ingredients (and the liqueur, if you like). Whisk the egg-whites to soft peaks, then add the spoonful of sugar. Use a little of this to slacken the almond mixture, then fold in the rest gently, so as not to lose too much air.

Spread the mixture on the baking parchment, in a rough circle. Bake on an oven tray for about 10 minutes – check after 5 – until it is pale golden brown. Remove it from the oven and leave it to cool on the parchment until you are ready to use it.

Bread Sauce

Bread sauce is one of those things you either love or hate. If like me you love it, you cannot imagine roast chicken or grouse without it.

Serves 4

1 small whole onion
6 whole cloves
150 g fresh breadcrumbs
500 ml milk
90 ml double cream
seasoning

Stick the cloves into the onion and put it in a small pan with the milk. Bring it to the boil and allow it to cool and infuse. Remove the onion and beat in the breadcrumbs, simmer for about 3 minutes and at the last minute stir in the cream and season to taste.

Brioche

This quantity makes two loaves. If you have a mixer with a dough hook, the process is much easier – but it is quite possible to do it by hand. Prepare it in the evening for the next day's breakfast.

625 g plain flour
45 g fresh yeast
40 g caster sugar
3 level teaspoons salt
6 eggs
225 g unsalted butter, softened
1 egg-yolk for glazing

Butter two loaf tins thoroughly and set them aside while you make the dough. Crumble the yeast and flour together in a bowl. Mix in the sugar and salt and then beat in the eggs, one by one, until they are well incorporated. Add the butter, one tablespoonful at a time. Beat (or knead) it thoroughly for a further 10 minutes.

Turn the dough out onto a lightly floured surface and cut it in two. Shape each half into a ball and tuck it into a tin. Leave it in a warm place for about an hour, to rise, and then put it into the fridge, wrapped in cling-film, overnight.

Oven 200C/ 400F/ Gas 6

Brush the surface of the loaves with egg-yolk, making sure that it doesn't touch the tin – which would inhibit rising – and bake them for 40 to 45 minutes.

Brown Stock

Ask your butcher to let you have some bones for this: it is particularly useful if they contain marrow. Use it for all beef and lamb dishes.

2 kg beef or veal bones
2 large onions, quartered
2 carrots, roughly chopped
2 bay leaves
1 dessertspoon black peppercorns
4 whole cloves
any available herbs

Oven 220C/425F/Gas 7

Roast one of the onions with the bones for about an hour – this length of time gives a good colour and flavour to the stock.

Put the bones and onion with everything else into a large pot and cover it all with water. Bring it to the boil and simmer it for about 4 hours, topping it up when necessary and skimming occasionally. Strain it and allow it to cool. Keep it in the fridge and discard the fat before using the stock.

Chicken Stock

This is the most useful stock of them all. You can make it with the bones of one chicken or of many, depending on circumstance. If you'd like the stock to look darker, roast the bones in a hot oven for an hour before you start.

the bones of one chicken
1 onion, roughly chopped
1 carrot, roughly chopped
1 stick celery, roughly chopped
2 sprigs parsley
2 sprigs thyme
2 bay leaves
1 teaspoon black peppercorns
1/2 bottle white wine

Put everything into a pan and cover it with water. Simmer for 4 hours, skimming occasionally, then strain it through a fine sieve and allow it to cool.

Clarified Butter

This is a very useful commodity. Unlike simple butter, it doesn't burn.

250 g butter

Melt the butter gently in a small pan. Allow it to cool a little until a milky residue has formed at the bottom. Pour off the pure butter into a bowl and store in the fridge until you need it.

Court-bouillon

This stock is sometimes known as a nage and is used to cook fish and in certain sauces.

2 onions
2 leeks
2 carrots
2 sticks celery
2 bay leaves
2 cloves garlic
2 pieces lemongrass
2 sprigs tarragon
2 sprigs parsley
1 dessertspoon black peppercorns
1/2 bottle white wine
11/2 litres water

Chop all the vegetables roughly. Put them in a large pan with the wine and bring it to the boil. Allow it to simmer for 5 minutes before adding the water and bringing it back to the boil, simmering it for a further half an hour, skimming occasionally. Leave it to cool before straining it.

Crème Pâtissière

This may be too much for the recipe you have in mind (e.g. Raspberry Soufflé) but it is very useful and keeps well in the fridge.

280 ml milk
25 g plain flour
2 teaspoons cornflour
4 egg-yolks
60 g caster sugar

Whisk the egg-yolks and sugar together and then add the cornflour and flour. Boil the milk and whisk it slowly into the egg mixture. Pour it into a clean pan and bring it slowly to the boil, until it thickens. Simmer it for a minute and then allow it to cool. Cover it with cling-film to prevent a skin from forming.

Fish Stock

The important thing about making stock from fish bones, as opposed to meat, is that it mustn't be cooked too long, or it goes cloudy.

2 kg cleaned bones, skins, heads, tails and fins of white fish
1/2 bulb fennel, roughly chopped
1 leek, roughly chopped
1 onion, roughly chopped
6 sprigs parsley
1 dessertspoon peppercorns
2 bay leaves
1/2 bottle white wine

If you are using fish heads be sure that the blood and liver have been removed before you start. Then cover everything with water and simmer for 20–30 minutes, skimming occasionally. Strain it through a fine sieve and allow it to cool.

Game Stock

This stock will depend on whatever is available to you. The ingredients suggested below should be seen as a guide – use your discretion, imagination and resourcefulness.

There is no need to peel the vegetables, just wash them.

2 kg carcasses from game birds
venison bones
2 large onions, quartered
2 large carrots, roughly chopped
4 mushrooms
4 cloves garlic
the tops from 2 leeks, chopped
4 stalks celery, chopped
6 sprigs parsley
1 dessertspoon black peppercorns
1 tablespoon juniper berries
4 bay leaves
1 bottle red wine

Oven 230C/ 450F/ Gas 8

Roast the bones for half an hour then put them with everything else into a large pot, cover it all with water, bring it to the boil and simmer it for 4 hours, skimming occasionally. Strain it and allow it to cool. Remove and discard the fat, once it is cold.

Hollandaise Sauce

This is enough to accompany asparagus, salmon etc. for four people. There are many apparently simpler ways to make a similar sauce but this is the very best and not, in fact, very difficult: once you've tried it, you won't want to lower your standards.

240 g unsalted butter, clarified (see page 147)
1 tablespoon white wine vinegar
3 tablespoons water
1 bay leaf
8 peppercorns
4 egg-yolks
juice of 1 lemon
salt

Combine the water and vinegar in a small pan, bring it to the boil and reduce it to one dessertspoonful. Allow it to cool, then put the pan into a barely simmering bain-marie and whisk in the egg yolks, allowing the mixture to thicken slowly while you continue to stir: take care not to turn it into scrambled egg. Remove the pan from the heat and add the clarified butter, little by little, stirring constantly and finally stir in the lemon juice and a good pinch of salt.

If you need to keep the sauce warm before serving leave it over the warm water, off the heat, and stir it occasionally to prevent it from curdling.

Lamb Stock

There are many sheep in the Islands and we find it useful to have this stock ready for casseroles and sauce.

2 kg lamb bones and scrag ends
1 onion, roughly chopped
1 leek, roughly chopped
1 carrot, roughly chopped
4 tomatoes, quartered
6 mushrooms
3 cloves garlic
2 stalks celery, roughly chopped
1 tablespoon tomato purée
1 dessertspoon black peppercorns
6 sprigs parsley
2 sprigs rosemary
4 bay leaves
1/2 bottle red wine

Oven 230C/ 450F/ Gas 8

Brown the lamb for about half an hour in the roasting tin with the onion, leek and carrot. Transfer them to a large pan and add all the other ingredients. Bring to the boil and simmer, to remove the acidity from the wine, then cover everything with water and allow it to simmer again, uncovered, for about 4 hours, skimming occasionally. Pass the stock through a fine sieve and allow it to cool. Remove and discard the layer of fat from the surface when it is cold.

Mayonnaise

This recipe provides the base for a variety of different flavours – herbs, lemon, caper, gherkin, garlic – really anything that takes your fancy. These flavourings should be stirred in, according to taste.

Serves 4

300 ml sunflower oil
2 egg-yolks
3/4 teaspoon salt
1 teaspoon Dijon mustard
juice of 1/2 lemon

Whisk the egg-yolks and mustard together, then add the oil very slowly, drop by drop at first. Add salt to taste and beat in the lemon juice.

To make saffron mayonnaise:
150 ml extra virgin olive oil
1 egg-yolk
1 clove garlic, very finely chopped
a pinch of saffron
salt

Steep the saffron in 1 dessertspoon of boiling water and leave it to stand. Beat the egg-yolk and add the olive oil, drop by drop. When it is all incorporated, add the saffron (with the water), the garlic and salt, to taste.

Pasta

This mixture is useful for all the pasta recipes in this book. It is wonderfully versatile: you can even deep-fry it in hot oil and use it for samosas, canapes and garnishes. You really need a pasta machine to make it, but you could use a rolling-pin, if you're blessed with a lot of elbow grease!

Serves 6

300 g white pasta/strong bread flour
3 egg-yolks
2 eggs
2 dessertspoons olive oil
pinch salt

Combine ingredients in a food-processor. Turn the mixture out onto a floured board and knead it lightly ∗, before cutting it into 8 pieces.

Roll each piece through the broadest mangle of a pasta machine 5 times to make sure the texture is smooth, then narrow the aperture until you have made long, broad ribbons and use it immediately.

∗ The mixture dries out quickly, so if you don't intend to use it at once, wrap it in cling-film at this point and keep it in the fridge.

Puff Pastry

The amount given here makes 700 g puff pastry, but I usually make double because, if you don't need to use it all at once, it will freeze very well. Reading this, it may seem to take a very long time to make, but each process only takes a few minutes. The finished product is very useful and much nicer than commercially available pastry.

375 g plain flour
340 g unsalted butter, at room temperature
10 g salt
110 ml water

Mix 250 g of the flour with the salt, 35 g of melted butter and the water in a bowl to make a dough. Shape it into a ball and cut a deep cross into the surface. Cover it with cling-film and put it into the fridge for half an hour. Beat the rest of the butter into the rest of the flour. Wrap this in the same way and put it into the fridge.

Remove the first parcel and put it onto a floured surface. Roll it from the middle into the shape of a four-leaved clover, keeping the centre part slightly thicker than the rest. Take out the other parcel and put it onto the central part, folding the clover leaves over the top. Roll this into a rectangular shape and fold it, from the sides, until it is in three layers.

Put it back into the fridge, on a floured tray, for a further half-hour then repeat the rolling and folding process again, twice. Return it to the fridge for at least two hours before you use it.

If you have any left over, do not scrunch it up into a ball but save it wrapped, in its layers, in the fridge or freezer.

Rich Shortcrust Pastry

It really is worth giving yourself enough time for this pastry to settle in the fridge before using it. It helps considerably to prevent it from shrinking during cooking. Though the quantities are unusual for shortcrust, they produce a marvellously versatile pastry to use with any fruit – or, if you omit the sugar, for savoury flans, pies, tarts etc.

240 g plain flour
170 g unsalted butter
1 dessertspoon icing sugar
1 egg-yolk
2 tablespoons cold water (if using Method 1) or
1 tablespoon cold water (if using Method 2)
a pinch of salt

Method 1:
Chop the cold butter roughly and put it into a food-processor with the flour. Zap it briefly until it looks like breadcrumbs then add the icing sugar and salt and give it another second of whizzing. Finally add the yolk and water, mixed, and continue just until it forms a ball. Take it out of the machine and put it onto a lightly-floured surface, taking care not to handle it too much. ✶

Method 2:
Allow the butter to soften at room temperature. Sift the flour with the icing sugar and salt onto a flat surface and make a well in the centre. Pour in the mixed yolk and water and draw the flour in slowly with your fingertips until it is well incorporated. ✶

✶ Wrap the ball of pastry in cling-film and put it into the fridge for half an hour.

Syrup no. 1

This is a simple syrup to be used for coulis and sorbets.

250 g caster sugar
250 ml water

Bring the ingredients to the boil, stirring throughout. Simmer it for 2 minutes and then allow it to cool. Keep it in the fridge until required.

Syrup no. 2

This syrup is useful for poaching fruit.

500 ml water
250 g caster sugar
1 vanilla pod (optional)

Bring all the ingredients to the boil, stirring throughout. Simmer it for a minute and then allow it to cool. Keep in the fridge.

Tapenade

This tasty and useful paste can be kept in the fridge for months and can be used for many recipes – canapes, sauces (for pasta) and toppings, for instance. It also makes a delicious dip.

200 g olives, pitted
50 g capers, drained
50 g anchovies, with oil
1 clove garlic
a good pinch of cayenne pepper
1 tablespoon good olive oil

Combine the first 5 ingredients in a food-processor, then add the olive oil. Store the paste, covered, in the fridge.

Tomato Sauce no. 1

750 g tomatoes, skinned, deseeded and chopped
1 tablespoon tomato purée
150 g cold unsalted butter
1 dessertspoon caster sugar
seasoning

Liquidise the tomatoes with the tomato purée and sieve the mixture into a saucepan. Heat it gently, without boiling and beat in the remaining ingredients.

Tomato Sauce no. 2

This can be used cold, as a salsa.

**1.5 kg tomatoes, skinned, deseeded and
    chopped
1 shallot, finely chopped
1 clove garlic, finely chopped
basil
extra virgin olive oil
seasoning**

Soften the garlic and shallot in the oil then add
the tomatoes, the basil and the seasoning and
simmer for a further 10 minutes.

Venison Stock

**1¹/₂ kg venison bones
2 onions, roughly chopped
2 carrots, roughly chopped
1 leek, roughly chopped
3 sticks celery, roughly chopped
4 tomatoes, quartered
4 mushrooms
2 cloves garlic
2 sprigs thyme
1 dessertspoon black peppercorns
1 tablespoon tomato purée
1 dessertspoon juniper berries
2 bay leaves
1 bottle red wine**

Oven 230C/ 450F/ Gas 8

Ask your butcher to chop the bones up roughly.
Roast them in a baking tin with the onions,
carrots and leek. When they are well browned,
transfer them to a large pan and add everything
else.

Bring to the boil and simmer for 5 minutes to
reduce the wine a little and add enough water to
cover the bones. Allow it to simmer, uncovered,
for 4 hours, skimming occasionally. Pass through
a fine sieve and allow it to cool. Remove and
discard the layer of fat that will form when it has
been in the fridge.

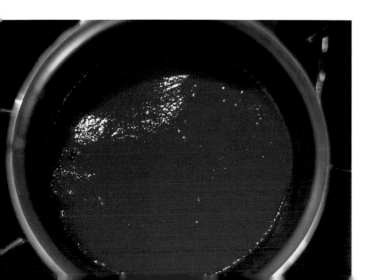

Vinaigrette

I like to keep a large jar of this readily to hand as it is so useful. If, however, this seems too much for you, merely halve the quantities.

250 ml olive oil
250 ml sunflower oil
100 ml white wine vinegar
1 teaspoon Dijon mustard
2 cloves garlic, peeled but not chopped
seasoning

Put the garlic into a screw-top jar. Mix the vinegar and mustard together and then add the two oils and seasoning to taste (a liquidiser is not essential, but it does produce a superb liaison). Pour it on top of the garlic and keep it in a cool place, but not the fridge. Shake it before use.

White Sauce

This simple sauce can be flavoured with anchovies, parsley, cheese, onions – almost anything you like. The important thing is to cook it long enough for it not to taste floury, and to keep stirring it so that it does not burn. Conventionally, equal quantities of flour and butter are used but I find that using a little more butter lessens the risk of lumps and makes a nicer sauce.

40 g unsalted butter
35 g plain flour
350 ml milk, warmed
seasoning

Melt the butter in a saucepan then remove it from the heat and stir in the flour. Return it to the heat and cook it for a minute, stirring it constantly and then add the milk, gradually, until it thickens. Allow it to simmer gently, as you stir, for another few minutes.

Amhuinnsuidhe Castle, home of Rosemary

Shrager's cookery school, stands sturdy, grey and crenel-
lated, facing the Sound of Taransay on the Isle of Harris. It
is a remote and isolated spot, part of a small Hebridean
community clinging to the furthermost limits of the
inhabited world.

A pleasing Norse legend about these Western Isles suggests an explan-
ation of their shape and position. The story goes that in the time of the
Norsemen they formed one large land-mass known as The Long Island. In
the hope of shifting the whole place nearer to Norway, the Vikings put a
rope through a hole in the cliffs at the Butt of Lewis and began towing it
home. All was going rather well until a mighty storm arose, snapping the
rope and breaking up the land into a scatter of islands. They settled where
they now lie off the north-west coast of Scotland, forming a short, curving
chain and dwindling in size towards the south.

On the map today they look a little like the skeleton of an antediluvian
fish. The largest of them, the head of the fish, is the Isle of Lewis. The Isle of
Harris is at the base of the skull: though connected to Lewis geographically,
its mountains are higher and its character subtly different. But there's one
thing that all these islands have in common: theirs is a largely oral tradition.
Hebridean history is passed down through generations, legend mingling
indissolubly with memory: generally untrammelled by dates, it is often
embroidered by hearsay and imagination. Now and again, however, a fact
or two can be established, particularly when tangible corroboration comes
unexpectedly to light.

One such piece of evidence surfaced in 1991 when some scallop-fishermen, working the waters off the eastern coast of Harris towards the Shiant islands, dredged up a remarkable catch. It was an exquisite torc dating from about 1000 BC. Made of gold which was probably mined in the Wicklow mountains of Ireland, it offered a tantalising glimpse of an ancient yet sophisticated and mobile society with a long and complex pedigree. Even with modern methods of communication, these islands can still seem wild and desolate from the perspective of cosmopolitan, mainland Britain – yet they have been inhabited for at least five thousand years.

Such history as can confidently be ascertained is long and often turbulent. Standing stones bear mute if enigmatic testimony to the importance of the place in Neolithic times, long before Christianity came to the Hebrides – and

stayed. The Viking empire held sway for four centuries before sovereignty moved to the Lords of the Isles, then away to the mainland and the royal houses of Scotland and, later, of England. Throughout most of this time, however, real power on the Isle of Harris was held by the Macleod family. Their formidable ancestor is thought to have been a Viking called Olvir the Unruly and many of their descendants still inhabit the island.

Amhuinnsuidhe Castle

Alexander, the last of the Macleods to own the island, disliked it. He chose to spend all his life and fortune in Edinburgh and upon his bankruptcy in 1834, the Isle of Harris was sold to the Earl of Dunmore.

Charles Adolphus, the seventh Earl of Dunmore, was a keen fisherman. Using the architect David Bryce he built his castle beside a secluded and beautiful bay, choosing a spot where a river, bursting with salmon, cascaded over rocks to the sea (Amhuinnsuidhe means 'sitting on the river' in Gaelic). Over three years from 1864–7, the Ayrshire stones of which it is constructed were shipped in from Glasgow, already cut and shaped, at enormous expense. Sadly, when the young earl showed it to his English bride, she was disappointed and claimed, they say, that her father's stable-block at Holkham Hall was bigger. To please her an extra wing was added, causing such acute financial embarrassment that, in 1868, the family had to sell the estate.

Of the subsequent owners, the Scotts are the most affectionately remembered, having cared for the estate and its families for many decades. Under their aegis many writers visited Amhuinnsuidhe, including J. M. Barrie who brought the four orphaned Llewellyn Davies boys here for two months during the summer of 1912. Lady Sophie Scott was particularly well-loved. Childless herself, she would send food and blankets to families with new babies and her children's parties are still fondly recalled. A pudding in this book is named after her, as is a pretty bedroom at Amhuinnsuidhe and her ashes, together with those of her husband, are in a cairn on the hill above the castle.

Life on Harris

Today the hills of Harris form one of the last great unspoiled wildernesses of Europe. Along the west coast broad beaches of silver sand sparkle against the clear turquoise waters of the Atlantic, often unmarked even by footprints. Beside these beaches lies the machair, the flat sandy coastal plain of peat onto which lime-rich shell-sand is regularly blown. For a brief spell every summer the machair blooms with a succession of wild flowers: daisies, buttercups, purple orchids and harebells. Strips of machair enriched by seaweed are carefully cultivated; lambing sheep graze it in spring before being herded

Opposite page, Calandish stone circle on the Isle of Lewis. *Above,* the castle. *Left,* a beach on Harris and undoubtedly one of the most beautiful in Europe.

up to the hills, as they have been for centuries; at one time to the sheilings, now to their summer grazing.

The Harrisman

Hamish Taylor was born on Harris in the house next door to where he now lives, on the rocky coast at Flodabay. As is the case with many of today's residents, he makes his living outside the traditional areas of crofting, tweed-weaving and fishing: he is a radio engineer, working with specialist radio navigation equipment for ships... and he is also an expert on seaweed. Occasionally he visits the cookery school to talk about the various types of seaweed to be found on the shores and to discuss their uses – most Harris people no longer use it directly for food, but dig it instead into the otherwise thin and unproductive soil.

Hamish is an Elder of the Church of Scotland. It is a broad church whose practices fluctuate according to local tradition. On Harris, strict Sunday observance is still the norm and many activities are discouraged. Another local custom ensures that Communion is celebrated only twice a year, always on the same Sundays in each village. When Hamish speaks of the traditional crofting year, he uses this as an example:

"Tradition matters a lot here. One family might always cut their seaweed on the first Tuesday after Finsbay Communion (that's near the beginning of March). I used to think such traditions quaint, but I respect them now. Bladder-wrack cut then, from the middle range of the tide, has time to decompose for a couple of weeks by which time you'd be ready to plant potatoes, to give them their best chance. Crofting families will be turning the ground with the seaweed and planting oats, too, during that time – and cabbages, carrots and turnips. There are fewer cattle to eat them these days, but oats are still grown – some for oatmeal, some for next year's seeds.

In May, the peat-cutting starts. We'll be handling it for the next few weeks. It's cut, then you lay it flat on the heather for three weeks. Then you build a small pyramid of four or five peats, with air-flow between them so that they dry for another month. Then you make bigger piles of them until they are dry and ready to take home in creels for winter fuel. In June, July and August the grass is growing, so we would cut it and make hay. In September and October it would be time to harvest the oats. The potatoes are ready too, but we have little frost here because of the Gulf Stream so they can wait, if they have to.

Sheep and cattle are the only animals we use traditionally: the ground is too steep and hard for horses. All the cultivation had to be done by spade and everything carried in a willow creel on your back. But traditionally every family had two milk cows and a few sheep, marked with colours and ear-tags.

As for fishing, there is a difference between summer and winter. Summer herring are very

fat and oily. They are excellent eating but no good for salting: they're too oily. In winter the herring come inshore to spawn, after the end of September. They are thinner then, and grand for salting. I've some in barrels now. People have always known easy ways to catch fish. You can see old fish-traps across most of our estuaries - low walls built at the place where the lagoon dries out every day, but where there'd be enough water for the fish to swim in with the tide and shoal. And then, as the tide fell and the fish began to worry, the wall would break the surface and they would be caught. It's using nature and working with it: both clever and passive. There were so many fish then that my mother would speak of not being able to sleep at night for the sound of jumping fish.

This fish-diet was high in calories and salt. People needed that because they were so active, to replace the salt they lost in sweat. So much salt did them less harm when they were doing so much manual work - and fishing still absorbs a fair proportion of men of working age here.

There is little poaching. There is a story of a rainy day when the wife of the then owner of Amhuinnsuidhe took her guests out with umbrellas onto the bridge near the castle, to

Opposite page, Hamish Taylor. *Above*, peat digging. *Right*, Kenny (in front) and Alec Morrison.

watch the salmon leaping up the falls. They looked downstream and there the fish were, leaping by the dozen. But when they turned to watch their progress upriver, they had disappeared. The answer was that a famous ghillie of the time was under the bridge waiting for the fish, with a gaff and a mail-bag! But there were plenty salmon to go round, anyway.

We say that if there were no watchers, there would be no poaching. Part of the fun when you're young is outwitting the watchers, up on the hills or beside the rivers. Besides, where some speak of poaching, my kind might speak of fishing, or hunting. There's a world of difference between doing it for financial gain and going out to fetch one for the pot – or to bait the ghillie! I remember there was one old ghillie who was also a watcher. He was called Big John Morrison. I went to see him when he was an old man in the hospital and I asked him: 'You know those nights you'd chase me all over the countryside – did you recognise who it was?' And he answered me straight away: 'Every time,' he said, 'and was I glad to see you.'"

Hamish speaks proudly of the islanders' famous reputation for scholarship. There is a higher per capita proportion of university graduates here than anywhere else in Scotland. He wonders whether it is because they have always had to use intelligence and common sense in order to look after themselves, to work alongside nature – or perhaps a diet of oily fish is really good for the brain.

He gives an example of this natural intelligence: in his photograph album is a picture of a man, spruced up in his Sunday best and smiling modestly. It is Murdo Macdonald. He lived right out in the wilderness between Huishnish and Uig. He went to school only one day in his life, in 1938, and that was to take his Highers. He got them all, including exams in Latin, Greek and Hebrew.'

Murdo's sister had taught him the alphabet. After that he learned everything by using the books carried on the Fleetwood trawlers which moored in the deep water at Loch Resort – they were his mobile library. "There is a minister still in Tarbert", says Hamish.

Below, time out on the hills. *Below right*, Murdo Macdonald.
Opposite page, Rosemary and Jonathan Bulmer examining the day's catch.

"Mr. Macrae, who's 82 now, and he passed his Highers on the same day. After Murdo passed, he'd intended to study Divinity at Aberdeen University. But he got sick and he was taken to Stornoway Hospital. And there, a doctor – a man who was highly trained – gave him the wrong medicine. And he didn't survive."

There's a lesson in that story and it could be this: given just a whiff of a fair chance, the inhabitants of this remote and physically challenging island easily take their place among the most highly motivated and resourceful people in the world.

The Landowner

Many of the residents of the tiny hamlet of Amhuinnsuidhe earn their living working at the castle or on the estate. The current owner, Jonathan Bulmer, has been in charge since 1995: it is he, in co-operation with Rosemary Shrager, who founded the famous cookery school. There he presides, a warm and generous host. He explains something of his passion for his home:

"The light in the Hebrides is a revelation. The poet Kathleen Raine once described it as 'a quality of the imagination'. There is a limpidity and cleanness in the air which is unique, even when the mist is down and rain sweeps horizontally across the hills. The ocean is never very far away and the great weather fronts drive in from the west. When the clouds lift and the hot sun burns away the mist from the hills and the lochs, the long, white beaches sparkle with the clarity and freshness of creation newly minted.

It is the sea, the endless Atlantic ocean stretching beyond comprehension to the west, that dominates. You see it from the top of every hill whose contours it has formed, you hear it in the dark winter nights and you

smell it on the warm summer breezes even in the deepest glens. It is the ocean that has shaped these islands and it dominates them still, lulling them summer-long in a sleepy embrace, chiding, chastising and terrifying with its winter storms, providing livelihood and taking life with equal invincible indifference.

For generations the sea, the sheep and cattle on the summer pastures, the potatoes and barley grown on the lazy beds near the shore and up into the hills, all sustained a way of life that was self-sufficient, proud and civilised. Donald Monro, High Dean of the Isles, writing in 1559 describes a country 'verey fertill and fruitfull for corne, store, and fisching,' and 'many forrests, querin are aboundance deir bot not grate quantitie, verey faire hunting games without any woodes, with infinite slaughter....'

The ancient Forest of Harris had been preserved for deer by the Macleods since time immemorial. Roddy Macleod, our head stalker, was born on the island of Scarp, as was his brother George; the Maclennans at Govig came from Scarp and Peter Dan ran his sheep at Kinloch Resort – it seems only the day before yesterday. The postman, now retired, recalls walking from Morsgail to Kinloch Resort and Hamnavay twice a week – a round trip of thirty miles – barefoot. St Kilda was evacuated in 1930, Scarp in 1971, Taransay in 1974, Deirascleit and Kinloch Resort in the 1950s. Their black- houses are roofless, their schoolhouses in ruins, visited only for the gathering and the dipping of sheep, their communities all finally defeated by the ineluctable demands of an industrialised and uncaring world. The

vast hinterland of moor and rock, hill and loch is now largely trackless, treeless, home only to the red deer, sheep, golden eagle, golden plover, divers, grouse and snipe.

We live by the sea and every year the miraculous run of sea trout and of salmon appears in the sea-lochs and in the bays. They gather, leaping and rolling and splashing in front of the castle. They lie in deep shoals nosing into the fresh water, their fins and tails breaking the surface like plangent kelp. With the first spates of June and then in July they surge up the rivers at Miavaig and Kinloch Resort and into the lochs, driven by the irresistible atavistic urge to regain the burns where they were born. It is primeval, it is awesome – and it is the start of our sporting season.

Every morning the ghillies in their Harris tweeds gather outside the rod-room to greet the guests. There is Roddy Macleod the head stalker, Kenny and Alec Morrison, brothers who have lived here all their lives (Kenny is married to the famous Effie who works with Rosemary in the kitchens), Innes Morrison, Roddy's stepson and Fiona's son and Malcolm Macinnes from Achmore. Tackle is sorted, decisions made and the parties depart for the lochs – by estate road for Scourst

and Vochimid or on foot for the hour's walk to Glinnhe or Ulladale or Mug's.

We fish the lochs from a rowing-boat, traditional, clinker-built, drifting with a rod casting from either end, rowed back at the end of the drift by the ghillie. This can be hard work, for the stiffer the breeze the more likely the salmon are to take. All the lochs are remote and wonderful places but each has its individual magic. Scourst is moody – sometimes dour and sometimes wonderfully productive, Alec's private kingdom; Vochimid the most famous of them all, where J.M. Barrie dreamed up his story of Mary Rose; Ulladale under its huge overhanging cliff where eagles can be seen and heard as they launch their young on their first, terrifying flights; Mug's, a longer walk to what is not much more than a pool in the river, where the running fish can rest.

Amhuinnsuidhe has always been a famous fishery. Its records go back over a century and very little has changed. The fish are still coming and we are still catching them. Although we have not suffered the disastrous declines of some parts of the Western Highlands where the sea trout have all but disappeared we are, these days, a great deal more environmentally conscious and on the whole return the fish we do not want to eat. We also have a Fishery Trust on the islands whose biologists monitor stocks and suggest ways of improving the habitat.

In September the stalking begins in earnest. We aim to cull about forty stags a year and the same number of hinds. This is to maintain the health of the herd and to prevent overgrazing. It is also the most exhilarating of all the days on the hill, a potent cocktail of physical exertion, nervous tension, sublime and ever-changing scenery and the best companionship in the world. The long spy, the slow climb. The inevitable checks and frustrations, the sudden rushes, the hair-raising chances taken and the suppressed excitement of the final approach create a bond between stalker and rifle that is palpable but unstated – at least until the shot is cleanly taken and the tensions dissolved in a dram.

Roddy and Kenny and Alec are intuitive stalkers. They have known every inch of the ground all their lives; they can sense every shift in the wind, every downdraught; how it eddies through a corrie or backs round a cliff and they know by a sixth sense where the deer will be and how they will move, when they will panic and run, when they will feed quietly on, where they will settle. They are patient, calmly reassuring and impressive in their knowledge and skill.

We no longer use ponies to bring back the beasts but drag or 'hump' them to the waiting vehicle. Humping is an old Hebridean tradition: after the gralloch, the stalker ropes the carcass on his shoulders and carries it downhill. The average weight of a stag is 11 stone 6, or 160 lbs. I have only tried this once, with a very small hind, and I managed about two hundred yards and was stiff for a week. There is no more elemental experience than lying up in a remote corrie, pinned down by hinds, while stags roar all around. Or dragging a hind back through the snow, with the full moon rising over Loch Vochimid. These are indeed the days.

There are grouse too at Amhuinnsuidhe, a population which fluctuates wildly according to the success of the breeding season; we

Above, the castle, in the background. *Right,* Sam and Effie peeling prawns outside the kitchens.
Far right, Rosemary with some of her students.

shoot them occasionally over pointing dogs, usually borrowed from Jim McGarrity at Aline. We rarely shoot more than ten or twelve brace in a day but it is always a joy to watch the dogs work and a welcome change from fishing in hot weather. Innes and Malcolm and the river-watchers do their best to control the feral mink who menace all the ground-nesting birds and take a terrible toll of juvenile fish.

The stags and the fishing finish in October. The winter months are spent catching up with the hinds, mending the roads (we have five miles of estate roads which are maintained every winter, literally by hand), repairing and repainting the boats and working on the fabric of the castle and the cottages. We also have a major replanting scheme in the garden and have recently planted 11,000 spring bulbs; thanks to the Gulf Stream there is nothing we could not grow here if we could keep out the salt and the wind, but that may take a long time.

The letting season used to be July, August, September and the first half of October. Now, with the cookery school, the painting and the music we are flat out from April to the end of October and employ up to 25 people, indoors and out, the vast majority of them local.

When I first moved to Amhuinnsuidhe I was asked why. I replied that I thought it was the loveliest place on earth. I still do and I believe, too – thanks to all my friends here who have worked so hard with so much laughter and good grace to make it possible – that we now have a future."

The Cookery School

The school was started in May 1999. Its purpose is to make the best use of both the magnificent raw ingredients provided by the island and waters surrounding it, and to pass on the unique and remarkable skills of the resident chef, teacher and passionate Harris-lover, Rosemary Shrager.

It is also a place of holiday and rest, where the anxieties and cares of bustling urban life can melt away in an atmosphere of timeless harmony – here with the season, the company, the island of Harris, and, of course, The Cook.

We are very grateful to Jonathan Bulmer, for his patience with this project and for the generous help and support he has given us, to Bridget Miller Mundy whose gentle tact and efficiency have been invaluable and to George Macdonald, Christine MacLeod and the rest of the team at the North Uist Estate office.

We would like to thank Margaret Hewitt and Fiona Macleod who keep the castle clean, comfortable and happy – and indeed all the rest of the staff, particularly Effie and Kenny Morrison and their marvellous family. Sam, a truly superb sous-chef, and her new husband Jonathan have been indispensable in the kitchens, helping us with remarkable, unfailing amiability, efficiency and good grace.

Others who have helped us on Harris are the kindly, invaluable Hamish Taylor; Bill Lawson, the genealogist and historian from Northton and Effie's uncle, Sandy Mackay. He and his charming wife Kirsty have run Amhuinnsuidhe Post Office for 50 years and shared with us their memories of working for the Scott family, long ago.

We are also grateful to Donald Norman Maclean, Ronnie Scott and Charles Macleod for keeping us supplied with fresh fish and meat and to Anderson Road Nurseries and Tony Robson for providing our delicious raspberries. We are grateful, too, to Andrew Farlie for his two excellent sous-chefs, Daren Campbell and Stevie McLaughlin, from *1 Devonshire Place*, Glasgow.

We tested many of these recipes over the millennial winter in East Sussex, where the following people were enormously supportive and produced superlative products for us: Clair Samuells, the splendid and resourceful fishmonger of Wadhurst; Chris Hillary, the magnificent butcher at Mayfield and the staff at Crittle's greengrocers, Wadhurst.

This book owes its very being to the vision, enthusiasm and commitment of David Campbell and the lovely Clémence Jacquinet at Everyman.

Finally, we are very grateful to our friends – especially to Kate and Philip Langford, whose generous hospitality knows no bounds – to our husbands, Michael and Rob, and to all our tolerant, tasting children.

Suppliers

I would like to recommend the following firms who supply their goods by mail order:

For fresh herbs:
Scotherbs,
Kingswell, Longforgan,
Near Dundee DD2 5HJ
Tel. 01382 360642

For fresh shellfish and flatfish
and for smoked salmon:
Ronnie Scott, Unit 2 Rigs Road,
Stornoway, Isle of Lewis HS1 2RF
Tel. 01851 706772

For Hebridean meat and, particularly,
black puddings:
Charles Macleod, Rope Work Park,
Stornoway, Isle of Lewis HS1 2LB
Tel. 01851 702445

For excellent cheeses:
Ian Mellis Cheesemonger,
205 Bruntsfield Place, Edinburgh, EH10 4DH
Tel. 0131 447 8889

For the finest peat-smoked salmon:
Mermaid Fish Supplies, Clachan,
Lochmaddy, North Uist HS6 5HD
Tel. 01876 580209

And finally, for the finest extra virgin olive oil
I am very grateful to my friends Simone and
Robert Benaim and to their olive tree farm,
Podere Sant'Antonio, Monte San Savino,
Arezzo, Tuscany, Italy.

Sam boils lobsters in the castle kitchen.

To find out about Rosemary Shrager's
Cookery School at Amhuinnsuidhe Castle,
please contact Christine MacLeod at the
Estate Office.

Tel. 01876 500 329
Fax 01876 500 428
E-mail: northuistestate@btinternet.com
Website: www.castlecook.com